WITHDRAWN

Individual Performer to Manager

A Practical Guide to Career Advancement into Management

A barefoot kid's journey from climbing coconut and guava trees in Hawaii, to climbing the corporate ladder.

By Norm E. Oshiro

Individual Performer to Manager

Published by:

Norm E. Oshiro
Cerritos, CA 90703
www.NormOshiro.com

Copyright 2018

First Printing, 2018

Printed in the United States of America

ISBN: **978-1729634837**

All rights reserved

No part of this book may be reproduced or transmitted in any form with the intention of reselling or distributing such copies without written permission from the publisher, except for brief quotations included in a review.

Cover design by Leslie Sears, www.lesismore.us

TABLE OF CONTENTS

DEDICATION V

PREFACE VII
    THE BOOK'S PURPOSE VII
    WHY AM I QUALIFIED TO WRITE THIS BOOK? IX
    BACKGROUND XIII

INTRODUCTION XV

CHAPTER 1: HOW TO SUCCEED AND EXCEL AS AN INDIVIDUAL PERFORMER 1
    MY KEY SUCCESS FACTORS FOR CAREER ADVANCEMENT AS AN INDIVIDUAL PERFORMER 2
    ATTRIBUTES OF A TOP PERFORMER 20
    DISCRETIONARY TIME AND SELF INVESTMENT 25
    TIPS FOR WORKING WITH YOUR MANAGER – WHAT YOUR MANAGER WANTS FROM YOU 27
    WHAT CAN YOU DO IF YOUR BOSS DOESN'T APPRECIATE YOU? 34
    BE A PROFESSIONAL OUTSIDE OF WORK 36

CHAPTER 2: EXPECT UNCOMFORTABLE, OVERWHELMING, EVEN TERRIFYING SITUATIONS 39
    DON'T QUIT 40
    TERRIFIED 41
    UNCOMFORTABLE 44
    HUMBLED AND DEMORALIZED, THE LOW POINT IN MY CAREER – MY STINT IN SALES 47
    BALANCING WORK AND PERSONAL TIME CAN BE DIFFICULT 53

CHAPTER 3: SO YOU WANT TO BE A MANAGER? 55
    YOUR JOB AS A MANAGER – KEY SUCCESS FACTORS FOR LEADERSHIP AND MANAGEMENT 59
    RESPONSIBILITY AND ACCOUNTABILITY 82

CHAPTER 4: MANAGEMENT RESPONSIBILITIES 89
    BUSINESS ETHICS 92
    HIRING AND FIRING 94
    REWARDS AND RECOGNITION 98
    RANKINGS AND COMPENSATION 102
    DEALING WITH COMPLAINTS AND DISCONTENT 116
    NOT FUNNY – A LITTLE DISRESPECTFUL 123
    AS THE HEAD OF A BUSINESS, YOU ESTABLISH THE WORK ENVIRONMENT AND CULTURE 125

CHAPTER 5: PROJECT MANAGEMENT 131

CHAPTER 6: WORST AND BEST 146

AMONG MY WORST EXPERIENCES AS A MANAGER	147
MY MOST REWARDING AND SATISFYING ASPECTS OF MANAGEMENT	152
CHAPTER 7: CLOSING	**157**
MY FIRST BIG BREAK	158
MAJOR INFLUENCERS	161
CAREER CHRONOLOGY	164
EDS LEADERSHIP TRAINING CLASSES ATTENDED (PARTIAL LIST)	167
EDS OPEN DOOR POLICY	168
EDS' GRASS ROOTS WISDOMS	169
SOME WORDS OF WISDOM WHILE GROWING UP IN HAWAII	171
CRITICISMS OF EDS	172
BIBLIOGRAPHY	174
ABOUT THE AUTHOR	175

DEDICATION

This book is dedicated to:

My Wife Carol:

In 1973, I lost both of my parents seven months apart. They were 49 years old, and I was 21. I was the only child, but after they died, I was never alone. From then on, my girlfriend at the time, Carol, took care of me and my shadow, my dog Shanti, whom she loved and cherished, and whom he adored in return. As of this writing, that was 46 years ago, we've been married for 45 years now, and we raised a son together. We've known each other growing up in Hilo since the 3rd grade. I would not be the person I am today, and I would not have achieved what I have achieved without Carol, my best friend, by my side every step of the way.

Cousin Byron:

Byron was three years younger than me. He was my kid brother and best friend growing up. We did everything together. We went to the drag races at Hawaii Raceway Park, we surfed together, and we rode our dirt bikes together on weekends. He was a proud Harley rider and longshoreman at the Port of Honolulu. We lost him to cancer in 2000 after a six-year fight. Not having him around today leaves a big hole in my life. We were supposed to get old together.

My Role Model and Mentor, Mary Buretta, from Electronic Data Systems (EDS):

Mary was the Account Manager for EDS' Seattle Systems Engineering (SE) Center, WA, and was the manager who first transferred me from Hawaii to the mainland in 1985. When reflecting on my career with EDS, I was extremely fortunate to have been offered that transfer position by Mary. Her entire staff and leadership team, the camaraderie, and the professional and supportive work environment I so enjoyed there was a reflection of Mary. It left an indelible impression which I carried with me throughout the rest of my career. Mary was my greatest EDS role model, mentor, and supporter, during my time in the Pacific Northwest, and for many years after I left, even after I became an SE Center Manager myself and we became peers for a short time. Even then, I still often turned to her for advice and guidance. I then reported to Mary again when she was promoted to Division Manager. We may have been peers for a while, but I was never close to her level of leadership.

I always held Mary in high esteem. Anyone who knew or worked with her would understand. She consistently had high expectations for quality work, she was commanding but not demanding, she engendered respect and admiration from her people, and I can still see her warm smile and light-hearted sense of humor, her openness and integrity, her compassion, and her unwavering strength of character to stand up for what is right, fair, and ethical.

PREFACE

The Book's Purpose

First and foremost, I want people to enhance their success as an individual performer, and to advance into management if they so choose. The topics that I cover; and the scenarios, examples, and advice that I provide; come from over 30 years of experience working for a large multinational information technology corporation, and working with people every day, in the trenches, as I progressed from an individual performer, to a team leader, supervisor, manager, to having a team of managers at a middle-management level, then to becoming a Project Manager exclusively. I discuss these topics on a very personal, experiential level, not from a typical business management textbook perspective.

When I started in the corporate world, especially since I came from a small town in Hawaii, I questioned whether I had the "right stuff" to keep advancing in my career or to even get into management. I'm hoping to reach people who think that they don't have the needed traits or aptitude, or may not be smart enough, or are too quiet and timid to progress to higher levels in their careers. If you feel this way, I want you to start recognizing and moving beyond your perceived limitations, and become more successful than you may have thought possible - including moving into the management arena. In this book, I describe my journey from an individual performer to getting into the throws of management. You'll read about the many difficulties I faced along the way, and hopefully be better aware and prepared to face similar challenges along your journey.

I provide tips and examples from a more personal perspective, on how I worked through these "limitations," became an increasingly valued individual performer, and progressively moved up the leadership ranks into managing larger teams and organizations. I never had that "executive look or presence" even at the height of my career, I was never a visionary, nor ambitious with a passion for reaching higher levels of management, nor was I a polished speaker or debater. Still, I was fortunate enough to have been hired by Electronic Data Systems (EDS), founded by Ross Perot, and I progressively advanced in the company. At the high point of my EDS organizational responsibility days, I had 190 people reporting to me, most of whom were Information Technology (IT) Systems Engineers (SEs), or Information Analysts & Specialists.

My motivation and drive to excel was not an early trait. It came with time on the job. I learned that everyone possesses more potential than they currently demonstrate – it just needs to be tapped and developed.

I also want this book to be a practical guide for people on how to improve as an individual performer as well as how to work their way into leadership and management, by describing what it will take to be successful from my own experience. Even if the reader has no desire to move into management, the topics on management should broaden the reader's perspective and understanding of that role, to help them advance further as an individual performer. If the reader is targeting a management career track, this book, through many examples, covers some of the key aspects that will help to prepare the reader to face many of these new challenges. I touch upon the great, the good, the bad, and the very ugly.

I was one of those who always feared failure, of screwing up, and who had to study really hard to get a "B," hopefully. I was one who when standing in front of an audience to give presentations, would be totally nervous, with shaky hands, and with a quivering voice no matter how many times I practiced.

It's still hard for me to believe, that a guy who went to school with bare feet through the sixth grade; who spent much of his childhood climbing guava, mango, and coconut trees; who hiked through pastures to swim in streams and ponds; who played with molten lava globs, and who hunted exotic fruits in the local rainforest; could somehow get hired by a big multinational corporation and work his way to attain the management level position that I did. So really, if I could do it.....

Why Am I Qualified to Write This Book?

After several decades of being a supervisor and manager, and having overseen many new employees come through the ranks as individual performers, I can look back at myself and reflect on some of the apparent qualities that I had through my years of trials and tribulations, that helped me to be successful. As I advanced in my career, I've had to coach people on what they needed to do to improve in their performance, and I've mentored individual performers as they moved into leadership. I've also observed people's shortcomings, how some have missed the mark, and how others could have upped their game.

I've had to rank people one above the other and be able to justify why when challenged during consolidations with other managers who had strong opinions regarding their people rankings. I've had to determine who deserved a raise or a bonus and the amounts, or who among a number of candidates, deserved a new opportunity or promotion.

I've also had to confront people regarding their performance or behavior, and I've had to let people go for consistently poor performance. In thinking back, I'm able to recognize how my work ethic or style, and some of my behaviors had allowed me to get noticed by management and as a result, given increasing opportunities to advance in my career.

In this book, I impart what I've observed and learned to hopefully benefit others who are seeking a more successful career as an individual performer or as a manager.

The guidance and tips I provide are from my recollections as an individual performer, and also from the perspective of having progressed over several decades to leading teams of people starting as a team leader, then supervisor, then a manager of supervisors, and then as a manager of managers. I had many people who were direct-reports to me, where I was directly and ultimately responsible for their project tasks, performance reviews, their development, compensation management, and their career progression. My position inherently carried a great deal of authority and influence over people when they are given assignments and have to accept direction and guidance.

From another perspective, in the last ten years with the company, I was in the role of a Project Manager where people did not report directly to me but were instead assigned or matrixed to me on specialized project teams, as with cross-functional teams. Also, these people were not on-site with me but rather from different locations in different states across the US. In these situations, you do not have the same level of "authority and control" as when people are direct-reports to you. You cannot directly "influence or maybe coerce" or hold them accountable for project deliverables with the same level of authority because you are not directly responsible for their performance reviews and you don't control their next promotion or salary increase or ranking. Their "real" managers do. So I had to develop skills and alternative methods to at times, exert extra influence to persuade certain people to complete their deliverables on time and per the requirements.

Writing this book is also from the perspective of having completed a formal and grueling 22-month Executive MBA (EMBA) program at the University of Southern California (USC), Marshall School of Business. I worked full-time throughout the program, and got minimal sleep. At the time, I was half-way through my 32 plus year career with EDS/Hewlett-Packard (HP purchased EDS in 2008).

In these writings, I capture my experiences and share them through many examples and scenarios. You'll find that although it covers some of the hard business management aspects, it covers more of the day-to-day interactions and challenges, and "soft" aspects, things that are generally not covered in an MBA program (which generally covers corporate finance, sales & marketing, organizational structure, global competition, etc.).

Finally, being a Sociologist affords me some sensitivity and insight into the interpersonal aspects in the examples and scenarios that I discuss.

The idea to write a book started in 2003. I first thought of writing something like a "management for the dummy" type of book, or "stuff they don't teach you in the MBA program." Since that time, I had been reviewing old notes and documenting recollections of experiences from the past, and in addition, jotting down noteworthy "teaching moments" as they occurred on the job. I ended up with pages upon pages of notes, culminating in this book, which actually represents less than half of what I've compiled so far. I had to call a stop and cut it off, or this book might have taken another year to complete.

Background

It's important to note that the material in this book is based upon my career with EDS, the company that Ross Perot founded in 1962.

I started with EDS in January of 1983, and retired from the company in 2015, 32 plus years later. Ross Perot' leadership, his customer focus, his discipline and compassion toward his employees, and his integrity and business ethics formed the cornerstone and served as the North Star for the company. I admired Ross the man (he did not want to be called Mr. Perot) and his leadership, and he was the reason I decided to move from Hawaii to the mainland after EDS lost the government contract to another company three years after I hired on. With the OK from Carol and our son Scott, who was eight years old at the time, we packed up with our two dogs, sold our house, and left Hawaii, where we were born and raised.

The EDS journey was hard, and at times very, very hard, with long working hours and weekend work, but I feel fortunate indeed, to have been a part of the growth and evolution of this company. I benefited tremendously from the leadership training I received; from the many dedicated, talented, and hard-working people with whom I worked; and from the coaching and mentoring I received from so many inspiring managers who took such good care of me over the many years.

I was also from a minority group, with a background very different from most in the corporation, particularly those in the leadership ranks. As an example, in my earlier years with the company back in the 1980s and early 1990s, there would be other minorities but I would always be the only Asian/Asian American in meetings or training classes back at corporate headquarters in Plano, Texas, or at EDS meetings in Michigan, Pennsylvania, Virginia, Colorado, and Utah. Many people were very outspoken, and I remember being ignored a lot, with people even avoiding making eye contact with me as we sat in class, or in groups or breakout sessions. Maybe they didn't know what to make of me at first. It most often ended just fine by the end of the meeting or class as we interacted and got to know one another. But those were situations where I thought: "what am I doing here?" and were quite intimidating at first.

As time went on, all of my EDS travels around the country were extremely positive. This encounter occurred while I was attending project meetings in Camp Hill, PA in the late 1980s.

> *It was some years after the Three Mile Island nuclear reactor accident where radioactive gasses were released into the environment. It was just 12 miles from the EDS offices. This EDS "old timer," who had worked for, and with Ross Perot personally for many years, was providing guidance on the Navy C2 project. He was up there in the company and the nicest guy, all 6' plus of him. One morning when I was the first person to join him in the conference room, we were chatting at the window, coffees in hand, looking in the direction of Three Mile Island. He was towering over me, and I asked him what it was like during the time of that accident. He looked down at me in all seriousness and said with his southern drawl, "Norm, before that accident, I was your size!" We busted out laughing, as more people started walking into the conference room.*

I consider my time with EDS as extremely fortuitous and feel grateful and proud to have been a part of this company.

INTRODUCTION

On a day after being absent in Mrs. Wessel's 3rd grade class (I was eight years old) at Riverside Elementary in Hilo on the Big Island of Hawaii, I came back to class to find that I needed to take a make-up test. After handing me the test, Mrs. Wessel and the class carried on as I sat there taking the written test. Then my friend and desk mate offered me a piece of paper under the desk, which was the test that the class took the day before but with all the answers. I had never cheated before and needless to say, I probably stood out like a sore thumb trying to look at the test answers under my desk. Well, Mrs. Wessel saw and immediately busted me with a loud shout, her chair slamming against the wall behind her as she quickly stood up, and thunderously stomped her way from her desk to me. Then she physically grabbed and lifted me to a standing position as she called me out for cheating.

That trauma of getting caught and being called out in front of the entire 3rd grade class was a significant emotional event and can best be described as putting the "fear of God" in me. It shook me to my core and stuck with me for the rest of my life. But what stuck with me as being just as bad and maybe even worse, is what I did when caught. In my panic, I pointed the finger at, and blamed my friend for giving me the answers. I suffered from the shame of being caught for cheating, and the guilt for blaming my friend.

But on that day, Mrs. Wessel became the best teacher I ever had in my entire life. I remember what she did like it was yesterday.

After the class settled down from the excitement a bit, she called me up to her desk, knowing that I was scared, shocked, and filled with guilt. When I got to her desk, she looked at me with overwhelming compassion, asked me if I had learned a very big lesson today, and if I was sorry for what I did.

I sheepishly and shamefully said 'yes,' then she said OK, and that she forgave me, and then told me to give her a big hug and to say to her 'I love you Mrs. Wessel.' So I did, and she responded in kind with a big firm hug of her own. At the time, I didn't know the words "compassion" and "forgiveness," but these words became more meaningful to me as I matured and reflected upon this day. I just knew it felt so good; I felt like I was forgiven, and knew that things were going to be OK. That's the kind of compassion that you can't learn from a dictionary, or by an explanation – you had to experience it.

But I never told my desk mate "thanks" for trying to help me, and I never said "I'm so sorry" for pointing the finger and blaming her when I got caught. The guilt bothers me to today, and I would give almost anything if I could go back in time and take that moment back.

Mrs. Wessel did not acknowledge or utter a word to, or about the person who offered me the test answers. I got a crystal clear message as to who was wrong.

I learned a very important and powerful lesson that day regarding honesty, integrity, and accountability; the impact of harsh consequences for my bad behavior; and the need to own up to my mistakes. Years later, it also showed me that as a leader, you have to promptly and firmly confront undesirable conduct, such as poor performance as well as bad or unprofessional behavior.

These and other difficult situations have to be handled by you personally, face-to-face and/or one-on-one. But equally as important, this experience constantly reminded me of the need to show forgiveness and compassion.

This life lesson from Mrs. Wessel shaped me as a person and as a manager. It impacted my overall management style, and how I treated people throughout my career and personal life.

CHAPTER 1:
HOW TO SUCCEED AND EXCEL AS AN INDIVIDUAL PERFORMER

My Key Success Factors for Career Advancement as an Individual Performer

1. My "successful career."

Since its subjective and extremely relative, let me first define what I'm considering to be a successful career for myself.

It feels like I'm being big-headed here but I needed to establish some reference point, so here goes. Remembering that I was an underperforming student from elementary school through my first year and a half in college, my "turnaround" started after switching majors from Engineering (yeah right!) to Sociology and becoming a research assistant at the University of Hawaii (UH) at Hilo in 1971 (see "My First Big Break" at the back of the book).

Then I went on as a graduate student and research assistant in Meteorology at UH Manoa, which is how I paid my way through grad school.

As I worked through the coursework, the Meteorology Department gave me ever-increasing responsibilities in laboratory and field research operations, and with an increasing team size to lead.

When I graduated with an MS, I was hired full-time as the department's Meteorology Field Manager for the University's 5-year Hawaii State Wind Energy research project and co-authored four UH research papers on wind energy potential for the state. When that federally funded project, and thus my employment, ended in late 1982, I applied to EDS and was hired in January 1983.

Over the years at EDS I progressed from a computer programmer Systems Engineer (SE) to Team Leader, SE Supervisor, SE Manager, Account Manager at a customer site, and then Account Manager of the 70-person Systems Engineering (SE) Center where I was based.

I was next promoted to Organization Manager, which was the highest level that I attained, where I had managers reporting to me, and eventually had the responsibility for multiple account teams and a total of 192 people in Southern California (see Career Chronology).

Following many years with the SE Center, and after acquiring an MBA while working full-time, I decided to broaden my corporate experience base, so I transferred into the EDS Sales Support organization. As it turned out, however, I did not do well in that group, but that's for another topic later in this book. After two years in Sales support, we were hit with a large corporate sales force reduction. I was impacted but was fortunate to be offered a transfer into the Government Services Group by a friend and former colleague, where I worked on a large US Navy contract based out of San Diego. I was able to continue with a successful and satisfying remainder of my career with EDS, this time as a project manager.

My work must have been well received because I continued to obtain very positive reviews from my peers and managers, I received salary increases and bonuses, promotions, and company stock options. In that time I also acquired two certifications, including a Project Management Institute's (PMI), Project Management Professional (PMP). I was planning to work another three years to the age of 66, but then, a generous early retirement package was offered to the older employees, and I decided to take it. I retired on May 31, 2015, at the age of 63.

So the above will be the reference point for my successful career. This "success" also includes what I consider to be a recovery from a less than successful two-year stint in sales support (again, more about that later).

Also, it's very important to point out that although I reference my college degrees, from EDS' perspective, degrees may have been important at corporate headquarters, but they were not critical out in the field and in the trenches. I was not hired because of my college degrees, I was not hired into a higher position or paid more for having a graduate degree, and I never got a raise or promotion for obtaining an MBA. EDS was always focused on results – not degrees, not "effort," not even seniority, but results. There was also no room for complacency in my experience with EDS.

2. The Context.

It's important to reiterate from my "Why Am I Qualified to Write This Book" section, that the recommendations I offer come from decades of progressing from an individual performer to being given increasing levels of responsibility, to ultimately having a team of managers as my direct-reports. Over these years, I've hired, developed, and mentored people, I've overseen their performance and career progression, and I've had to assess their contributions and value and had to rank them with clear justifications. I've managed their compensation, I've had to confront people on performance issues, and I've praised and rewarded people for their good work and contributions.

As I reflect on my career, I can see how my work ethic/style and some of my strengths have apparently served me well. They not only earned me advancements and new opportunities but also allowed me to survive a significant number of corporate down-sizings where I witnessed many colleagues being laid off around me.

So with that context, the following are my recommendations for success and career advancement.

3. Work hard and give it your all.

It was never part of my younger nature, but I somehow developed this willingness to work really hard. This was a key aspect of my getting ahead and being given more responsibility and more opportunities over the years.

That meant following through with any assigned work, no matter how difficult or unfamiliar, or undesirable it might have been, and getting it done successfully. I was willing to work long hours, meaning staying after regular work hours, and also bringing the work home with me for evening or weekend work if needed to complete an assignment or get further ahead.

I always did this without the expectation of getting any comp time (compensatory time off). It also meant doing a lot of studying on my own time, on what might have been a new subject matter due to having been given some new responsibilities. Believe it or not, one of my stress relievers was to think and realize that if I couldn't get this done at work today, I could stay up all night working on it if I had to. I had done that many times cramming in college. (I also discuss work/family balance later.)

But in addition to working hard, you need to look up from the daily grind and look ahead to what else is needed by your team, and strive to bring more value, to be more helpful, and try to become a resource who is often sought out.

4. Always take on your assignments with a sense of urgency.

Don't be rushed, or rude to your co-workers, or be bouncing off the walls, but don't always casually stand around shooting the breeze either. You need to be absorbed in your assignment, researching, asking questions, working with purpose, moving sharply, and always focused on getting results.

You need to keep your leader apprised by providing your manager/supervisor/team leader with updates and progress reports without always having to be asked – the greater the importance, the greater the frequency. This will demonstrate that you are taking your assignment seriously and want to do it well.

You'll get a feel for when the frequency is becoming less necessary – generally because the confidence you are instilling in your leader is growing, and their level of concern is decreasing.

Be careful not to become a frequent visitor either, like you are constantly looking for approval – it's a balancing act.

5. Hustle.

Don't walk around like you have all the time in the world. It looks like you don't have enough to do. Hustle. Move sharply, briskly, not rushing, but like you have a purpose.

> *My brother-in-law, who is a high school and old surfing friend, and who is a retired carpenter and stone mason, once told me that a long time ago, this old Japanese carpenter foreman told him that he would watch as new workers parked their cars, grabbed their tools, and walked on to the job site. After many years of running crews, he could immediately tell by their movements which ones would be the good workers and which ones would not. He ultimately hired and chose not to hire some people based on how they geared up and walked up to the job site.*

I learned to "hustle" from playing baseball as a kid. I played for many years for my local Boys' Club team – from T-ball to Little League through Pony, Colt, and some Senior League. You never walk onto or off the field, to and from your position – you don't necessarily do the 100-yard dash, but you run or jog it – you "hustle" out. If you don't hustle, you're not serious. I later realized how much of an impact this had on the rest of my life – mental attitude and preparedness, also as viewed by others, when you move with purpose.

6. Be reliable and give your best effort – always.

Always come through with your assigned work. Always meet your commitments. Always be there and give it your all when your team needs you. I had a tiny bit of experience with outrigger canoe paddling in Hawaii, but have friends who are very experienced paddlers. When you are paddling, you are the engine for the canoe, you provide the forward thrust to reach your destination or the finish line, and you can't hide giving only 90%.

One of the main things you are taught, and you learn very quickly on a six-man crew, "braddah, you betta pull yo own weight or get off"!

Even if people can't see the work that you're doing, it eventually becomes obvious who are pulling 100%, and who are not.

7. Don't decline an assignment, challenge, or opportunity, no matter how ill-prepared or unqualified you think you may be.

If you are tapped, someone thinks you can do the job, or there may be no one better than you who can handle it, from your leadership's assessment. I never declined an assignment.

There were times where I had great reluctance, where I felt and even argued that I was not qualified, and once felt that a job was extremely undesirable and I requested that it not be assigned to me. But ultimately these assignments were never withdrawn, and I never turned one down. One such assignment was to become the account's "Quality Manager" which was during the early 1990s when Quality Improvement & Total Quality Management, and "doing it right the first time and exceeding customer expectations" became the mantra for most companies.

This was one assignment where I had to do a complete "mind-shift" from perceiving it as an extremely undesirable assignment, to fully embracing it, and taking it on 110%. I got formally trained (Crosby) and became the enthusiastic driver and spokesperson for the effort for the entire account. It was a valuable learning experience, and it was a stepping stone to more and bigger opportunities. As an individual performer, or team leader, or manager, you'll inevitably get assignments you don't want or think you can't handle. You'll decide to decline it, or accept it but perform the job reluctantly, or embrace it and give it your all. Your approach and mental attitude will always be under your control.

So don't automatically turn down opportunities and assignments because you think you can't handle it. I've had situations where I've said "you're kidding right?" thinking the task was way beyond my capabilities and experience level.

You have to be willing to take risks to accept more responsibility and greater challenges. I also had great managers who kept persisting, but also continued with their encouragement and support for me – even if they had reached the very bottom of the barrel.

8. Never quit, no matter how bad it seems – things somehow, always tend to work out.

When I first started with EDS, I can still remember my first project working for the US Army Corps of Engineers, on a Hydro Survey project. I found the work so complex that one day I broke out in a cold sweat and my heart racing, thinking what am I doing here – I can't do this work.

On another occasion, when I was a newly minted SE Supervisor, I had to do a performance review for a retired Navy Lieutenant Commander and go over the required "things you need to do to improve." I also had to give a few stand-up EDS leadership classes to a room full of older and way more experienced managers at one of the companies that EDS acquired, where I was incredibly intimidated and visibly nervous.

And among the worst of all, early in my career when I was still a supervisor, I was brought in as the account manager to run the IT department for an aluminum wheel manufacturer. One day soon after I got there, I asked my primary customer, the plant manager, if I could attend his management meetings. He responded to my face, "it wasn't my decision, and I didn't agree to hire EDS, I don't want EDS here, and no, you can't come to my management meetings."

That was how we started out. I was there for two years, and I got along well with everyone but the plant manager. Things did get better, but I never was invited to his management meetings.

So in your career, things will never always be easy, and they may often be extremely difficult, but keep at it and push through it. If it somehow turns out to not work out, then learn from it, so you'll be better prepared for your next challenge. In the long run, it'll be blips on the radar, like all the above turned out for me, and you'll be better for them.

9. To increase your value, always be willing to invest in yourself.

Throughout my career, I spent many hours of my own time studying technical as well as management/leadership material. When I saw a clear need to better position myself to be more productive, I never waited for the company to provide me with all the necessary equipment or training. EDS provided a lot of excellent technical and leadership training, but I also went to the library, purchased books, read periodicals, and even purchased PCs, which were new at the time, to learn to program as well as how to use the software.

Way back in college, I acquired a modem to connect to the University mainframe at a blazing 300 baud, then applied these types of new found knowledge at work. I did this before EDS and throughout my 32 plus year career with the company. While working for the University of Hawaii, I purchased an Apple II+ computer (with 48K baby!), so I could study microcomputers and programming on my own.

After I joined EDS, in the evenings, I studied VisiCalc (spreadsheet) and VisiPlot (graphing), so I could become proficient and teach others at work including our customers. When the IBM PCs came out, I did the same with Lotus 1-2-3 and WordPerfect.

The main point is that besides employer-provided tools and training, I always spent my own time and money to invest in myself, from hardware/software tools, to books on technology as well as on business and leadership. I also attended a few classes put on by training companies outside of EDS. I was reimbursed for some expenses, but if I could afford something I thought I needed, whether or not it could be reimbursed was never a determining factor. And if I had minimal dollars to spend, I still would have figured out ways to learn new things to help me at work.

The result was my being able to bring added value to the team, the customer, and the workplace. Your willingness to invest in yourself becomes apparent to co-workers and your manager because they'll notice that you have more knowledge and abilities than they may have thought.

10. Be friendly and courteous.

I always made a point to be friendly and courteous to all the people with whom I worked. Being able to get along with others has always been a key aspect of my having a successful career, and it helped to foster an overall positive office environment.

I always made eye contact and greeted people with "good morning," always offered a smile and said hi or at least gave a friendly nod in the hallways. The same for "good night" when leaving for the day. What made a significant impact on me relating to this was on my leaving the Seattle SE Center, where I spent a year and a half after transferring from Hawaii, and I received such a warm and memorable send-off. Even the few people who maybe were overly shy, and who would rarely make eye contact or say hi to me in the hallways, said such nice things in the large Going Away Card that was presented to me (and which I've kept and treasured all these years), saying how much they appreciated my friendliness. It was only then that I realized that my friendly nature was indeed making a positive impact, and this was incredibly rewarding.

But remember, first and foremost, you need to do your job well, and you need the respect of your peers. If you are a consistently poor performer and can't be depended upon by your team, being friendly and courteous won't make up for it.

11. Offer to help and actually do something.

I was always willing to roll up my sleeves and help anyone who needed assistance. If you've figured out how to solve a problem or to increase productivity, or if you see someone else having a hard time, always be willing to lend a hand. When things are hectic, maybe due to a project deadline or emergency, when the pressure is on to get work done, when people around you are busy, never, ever, stand around, and never, ever, ever just stand around talking.

See/assess what people are doing, search for something that you can do. Offer to help, and don't take "no" for an answer. Insist, or instead of asking "how can I help?" ask "what can I do?" or "give me something to do" or "tell me what I can do." Maybe people are busy setting up tables and chairs for an urgent meeting, or cleaning up after a gathering, so it's easy to lend a hand. Or maybe there's a project crisis of some sort, but you don't have the needed expertise and want to help the team.

So go get them something to drink from the break room, go make copies or pick up printouts, help clear off a table so they have more space in the war room – there's almost always something to do to help. Less talk, more work. Then also, if necessary, get out of the way, but tell them you're ready to help and to call you if they need anything.

12. Do your homework to always be prepared for meetings.

This is where your visibility to the entire team and your leadership starts. It generally begins with providing a status report on your assigned tasks.

Always be respectful of people's time and provide a concise summary (so write it down) on what you're doing, what you've accomplished, what problems or concerns you are having, and what actions you are taking to address them. This means you've already done some research on the problem, starting with asking your teammates, on how to resolve the problem.

Maybe you want to present it to the group to ask if anyone has seen this before and might have a solution or some ideas, where you can then take it "offline" and get together after the meeting. I was always motivated to be prepared because I hated to be seen as being unprepared, or being caught flat-footed, and unable to answer some basic questions about my assignments.

If I had a problem, I wanted to be able to lay out what I was already doing or what plans I had to work through the roadblock. Again, be concise, which means you took some time to prepare, and never meander, unless you like to see, or maybe not see, people rolling their eyes behind you.

13. Don't try to BS people if you don't know something.

I remember way back when I first started with EDS in Hawaii at the Fort Shafter US Army Base; there was an older, highly regarded IT consultant contractor from another company supporting the Army.

He was known as a top-notch person around the IT community on base. In my first contact with him, I was fairly intimidated because he was a reputable professional and I was a younger, inexperienced person, and we were from competing contracting companies.

We were in a meeting with the customer, and he asked me something on some technical matter which I probably should have known, but as much as I hated to, I had to say I didn't know the answer. He asked "you don't know?" where I responded with "sorry, no." But as it turned out, he apparently admired that I didn't try to BS my way out of that situation, and I was instead honest about it. He knew I was green, but we ended up having a good professional relationship from that point on.

You have to be open and honest – people will know if you're BSing, and you'll lose some credibility when you do.

14. Don't stop work and go home because it's 5 o'clock.

One of the things I learned with EDS, especially in the earlier days, is that if there is a critical, project or customer-impacting problem, you don't stop work and go home at 5 pm. The project deadline has to be met, or the live production application glitch has to be fixed, so you work until the problem is solved, or the work is completed. If you have some breathing room, you still don't leave until you've at least figured out a path forward and know what actions you need to take the next morning.

In my experience, in the earlier days, this was the rule rather than the exception. Things improved over time with more reasonable sales deals/contracts and better project management, but emergencies come up, no matter how hard you try to prevent it, so you have to be ready to pitch in with some long hours, late nights, and weekends at times.

Management needs to recognize and appreciate these efforts, and never take it for granted, or there will be a high turn-over rate.

Of course, if you have other commitments, family or otherwise, it will be your judgment call. See the "Balancing Work and Personal Time" topic later.

15. Get to work early.

If not all the time, then at least sometimes. You can get a lot done before the daily chaos starts. If I didn't get to it the night before, this is where I got through my email and did any needed critical planning.

16. Always dress neatly.

For me, it was never the most expensive or fashionable clothes, but I always tried to look sharp and clean. In the business suit days, I made sure my tie was pushed neatly and firmly up to the top button of my dress shirt. I made sure that my tie was never exposed from my collar at the back of my neck, and jacket sleeves were at the proper length (never have sleeves too long or too short!). I kept my dress shirt neatly tucked and never hanging out, trousers not too baggy, too long, or too short, and smart shoes (wingtips back then) – not always spit polished but never dull and scuffed.

This still applies to today's business casual, casual Fridays, Aloha Fridays, or jeans casual dress – be neat and clean, and never look sloppy. Most people will take notice, and it makes a difference in how you are perceived personally and professionally.

To give you an example of how strict EDS' dress code used to be when business suits with long-sleeved (not short-sleeved) dress shirts were required. For the men you could take your suit top (jacket) off while working at your desk, but you could not leave your cubicle or office and walk in the hallways without it – yup it really used to be that strict, and that was in every EDS office anywhere in the country (except Hawaii, where I was hired, where suits were not appropriate). You also could not wear shoes with tassels.

> *I remember on my first visit to EDS' corporate headquarters in Plano, Texas when I went to lunch with my colleagues to the cafeteria. Before sitting down, I instinctively took my suit jacket off and put it on my seat back. I happened to look around and immediately noticed that I was the only one in the entire cafeteria with hundreds of employees without my jacket on, so I quickly made the correction.*

If you were a woman, you could be sent home to change if your skirt was a little too short, or if your top was a little too revealing. Once one of our more senior SEs spilled a glob of spaghetti sauce on his white dress shirt at lunch. He drove 30 minutes to get home to change before returning and stepping back into the office. Yup, for real. That was the dress culture.

17. Make sure you have good writing skills.

Your capabilities and professionalism will also be judged by your writing skills.

Make sure you pick up good writing skills and use your spelling and grammar apps.

If you think you need some assistance, there are a number of online apps now that will check your writing and grammar, and offer corrections with explanations. You can use these to double-check your emails, your status reports, project debriefs, and formal reports and documentation, so do some homework and take advantage of these tools.

Poor writing skills reflect badly on you and your level of professionalism.

18. Be calm, relaxed, and poised.

OK, I was never tall and handsome (well not tall anyway...) – never had a strong or commanding physical presence, nor ever had that "executive presence." But I was able to dress neatly and professionally, stand with a good confident posture, all 5' 3" of me, well OK, 5' 1 3/4", close enough, and hopefully projecting some level of confidence with a calm demeanor.

I had learned how to stand straight, feet slightly apart, head straight, back straight, shoulders down, hands to the side or folded in the front or back, breathe with mouth closed, and try to be poised but relaxed.

This is through some training on physical coordination and presence, and how to carry yourself, like in sports, or gymnastics, dance, or even business etiquette classes.

Never stand hunched, leaning against something, with your hands in your pockets, or with your mouth open, especially in a professional setting.

19. Be "low maintenance."

In-other-words, don't be a constant complainer. I spent more time getting my work done, or trying to resolve problems, rather than creating problems or complaining to my manager. If you see problems, don't go running to your manager to point them out, thinking you're a hero for discovering it, unless of course, it's urgent or an emergency.

If at all possible, give thought to how it could be fixed. Think of alternative solutions that you could present as well. Offer to help with the solution if you can. Just don't be the person who only "finds" problems. Similarly, don't always go running to your manager looking for attention and approval.

There's an appropriate time to socialize with your manager, to joke around, or get to know one another better, but more often than not, time spent with your manager should be to get results that advance the project or to achieve important goals.

20. Don't bad-mouth people, especially your manager.

Some people get a kick from getting laughs or attention by criticizing or bad-mouthing others. But remember, if they like to bad-mouth people, they're probably bad-mouthing you when you're not around.

If there is some problem that is negatively impacting the team or the project, then address it with the person, or your manager, or your manager's manager.

If it has more to do with idle criticism or back-biting, then better to keep it to yourself or you'll earn the reputation of "talking behind people's back."

21. Be efficient and productive.

When I was the field manager for the Hawaii wind energy effort at UH, around the early 1980s, I was at the motor pool one day getting our research van repaired when a University facilities person drove up with his backhoe requesting some repairs. He said the backhoe arm was working, but the hydraulic action was too slow. He said it was costing him productivity and taking longer to get his work done.

Go figure, but this made a big impact on me. It highlighted the importance and value of speed and accuracy in doing your job.

From that point on, I was always conscious of how things could be done faster, or what things were slowing things down, from the setup and even the positioning of tools, to the setup of things on my desk, or being able to type faster on the keyboard, or learning to use short-cut keys for software applications, etc.

On my current desktop/laptop mouse, for example, I can actually cut, copy, paste, enter, double-click, tab forward, and go back, all with single action button clicks without the right click first.

And why count to three when taking everyone's picture? Count to only two instead, and you save everyone one second. I don't actually do this picture thing, but you get my point.

22. Always take notes.

Taking notes is how you make sure you don't miss anything important.

It also shows that you are focused on listening and trying to understand.

Review your notes to assess and plan, then take actions and follow-up to completion. I have log books, like composition books, which go back to my college days – a lesson from doing research. I also have for every year, the accompanying calendar books, like the week-at-a-glance series, showing my meetings, appointments, and key events. Once as a Project Manager, I had a person assigned to me who I shockingly found, didn't take notes as we're gathering information and requirements. So I'm thinking, OK, he must have a photographic memory or something. Well, that was not the case, and important things were missed.

It confirmed my thinking that if you don't take notes, you're not serious about capturing important information for the project, so I would prefer not to have you on my team.

23. Extreme fear of failure.

This topic is a little different relative to being a success factor, in that you either have it or you don't through your life experience, but this was indeed a critical success factor for me.

I primarily obtained this fear from my little league days. The net of it is that I hated making errors, I made quite a few of them, and I made some critical errors that cost us those games, and two of them were championships. I can still hear the huge crowd cheering with excitement as the ball is hit, and the loud disappointing "awe's" when I made those errors. Walking back into the dugout and seeing the disappointed coach and my teammates, and even all the parents out there was devastating.

My parents trying to comfort me did not help one bit. I also remember the progression from the time that the coach thought of me as one of his top players, to becoming disappointed with my level of play over a few years to where he had to move me from the infield to the outfield.

I still remember that day when he had to tell me that he was moving me from third base to left field. I must have shown a real let-down because I remember him saying that he needed somebody good that he could trust in the outfield as well. I actually did much better at left field, I never made an error in that position, but still, it was obvious to everyone that this was a big demotion.

Similarly, my batting position dropped from being 1st or 2nd in the lineup to 8th and 9th. It was heart-wrenching to see my value keep dropping on the team. All this was when I was 11 and 12 years old, but these memories got burned in and affected me throughout my career.

And of course it's not just the failure, it's the hurt and shame of letting people important to you down – your teammates, coach, family, then shifting that to the workplace, the fear of letting down my co-workers, managers, and customers.

At work, I never felt like I was competing with anyone else for the next promotion or opportunity – that was never a motivator for me. What drove me was the extreme fear of failing and letting people down.

> *Bear with me for a minute here. There's a scene in the movie "Moneyball" where Chris Pratt (Guardians of the Galaxy) is in the break room and is asked by one of the veteran players "well what's your biggest fear?" Pratt responds with "the baseball being hit in my general direction," where the two of them then laugh. So the veteran asks again, "seriously, what is it?" Pratt then stops laughing, his expression changes to one of concern, and says, "no seriously, that's it" then slowly turns and walks out of the breakroom.*

That exactly describes my feeling when I was playing baseball back then. Every time a batter was up at the plate, I was deathly afraid that he was going to hit the ball in my direction, and I would make an error. Now how sad is that, but it says something about how my self-image and self-confidence was shaped. Having faced these failures and letting people down made a huge impact on me, but I would not change any of it. I love baseball today, and I'm still pretty OK at it even at my age, but these experiences made me who I am. It gave me great empathy towards others facing similar situations. It gave me a heightened awareness and need to work as a team, to share successes as a team, and to have tolerance, patience, acceptance, and inclusion towards others.

A simple "that's ok" after someone makes a mistake can mean a lot and help them feel better about themselves.

This is why I get so upset when I see people being put down, or being made fun of, or being ill-treated in any way. I've been on the receiving end of these.

24. Being a workaholic is not a requirement to be successful.

It's important to note that consistently or incessantly working long hours and weekends is not a requirement to be successful.

I have had the good fortune of working with many others, including managers, who maintained a much better balance of work and home life than I ever did, and who were among my top performers. I would not have achieved what I did without them.

Maybe I wasn't as quick to pick things up, or as productive in getting things done, but working all those long hours, for all those years, was my choice, and as I see it, was essential for me to have achieved the level of success that I did. I am certain that for me, if I had throttled back from my level of effort, I would not have attained the same level of success. In that time I did reach a relatively high management level, and I was compensated well, both when I was an organizational manager with many people reporting to me, then as a senior level project manager, when I had no one formally reporting to me.

So to reiterate, you don't have to always put in crazy long hours to be successful. You can maintain good work and personal balance and be respected by your peers and managers.

But you still have to be very productive, work with a sense of urgency, be reliable, constantly increase your value, be low maintenance, have good writing skills, be prepared and concise in meetings, etc.

See the section "Balancing Work and Personal Time Can be Difficult" in Chapter 2 for more on this topic.

Attributes of a Top Performer

1. **In my years of experience, I've found that the people I'd consider among the very top performers made up roughly 10% of the organization, and they consistently demonstrated the following:**
    - An extensive track record of successes and accomplishments on the most difficult and complex tasks or projects.
        - I've found that even given work in a new area or subject matter, the top performers would quickly and consistently become one of the best performers in that new area. It might be a new technology, new programming language, or a new industry (insurance, financial, manufacturing, airline, government, etc.) that we were supporting.
    - Excels in many areas.
    - Has a sense of urgency in getting their work done.
    - Highly productive – fast and accurate and gets a lot done.
    - Has the respect of their customers, peers, and managers.
    - Project managers want them on their team, especially for high priority/visibility projects.
    - Very proactive, anticipates problems and alerts people ahead of time, has the initiative to take action, or pulls together others to put things in place to avoid or address problems.
    - Talks less and works more to produce excellent results – not to be anti-social, but there's a time for chatting as well as an appropriate amount.
    - Motivates others by example.
    - Has a knack for tasking others and tracking progress.

- Stays when the clock hits 5, and critical work still needs to get done.
    - Some people had priorities where leaving at 5 was non-negotiable due to family or other obligations, and that was expected, but understandably the ones who consistently stayed to get crucial work done generally contributed more, and usually ended up ranked higher.
    - I say "usually" ranked higher because it's important to remember that the level of "effort" or long hours put in by someone, does not necessarily translate into making the biggest impact or producing the best results. One of my heart-wrenching actions as a supervisor was having to separate (fire) an employee who was among the hardest workers and who put in the longest hours, but who was not producing good results.
    - I also had an employee who was always among the top performers and highly ranked, who had young children, and who set her parameters to leave at a specific time every day. This also meant that she had a number of maternity leaves which turned out to be non-issues at work. To be clear, there were many more women and men, with young children, who did not set such parameters and who worked very long hours. This individual could rarely work on weekends, even for critical deliverables, but never-the-less, she was such a focused and high output/impact employee that she was always critical to a project's success. If she could not be at work, she would map out what needed to be done, identify the best person or persons to do it, and prepped with the person(s) so the needed tasks got done. Even when she chose to go to 3/4 time, her impact was still high and although a number of people overtook her in the rankings, and only because she was not full time, she was still a highly ranked/rated person. She remained a top pick for any project.
- Lastly, there were high-value people who were consistently willing to travel on extended temporary duty assignments (TDY) out of town, or out of the country, to support our customers. They endured months of living in hotels or

apartments, many away from their families, eating out, some traveling back home on the weekends, others regularly visiting the laundromats, then having to also deal with travel arrangements, rental cars, expense reports, etc. Some would come back from one long TDY, and with another critical customer support need, be willing to go right back out on another long TDY assignment. They were our road warriors, and they were critical to our SE Center's success.

2. Exceptional performers?

- Your top performers will be able to point to your exceptional performers.
- Give them the toughest most complex jobs, and you can just about forget about it – they'll let you know when it's done.
- They excel in their technical abilities, may have no interest in going the management path, but have the leadership and project management skills to pull a team together, assign the work, keep everyone on task, and make sure everything gets done on time.
    - o I had a person like this who was assigned to me for a new project many years ago before even Project Management software tools were common, and on very short notice, he took this priority project, which was also a TDY assignment in another State, with a team of about 8 people, and carried it through to successful completion. Just one more of many for this person.
    - o Midway through that project, on a trip back to the office, he provided me a status, then showed me how he was managing the project with hand-written notes on a few sheets of yellow pad paper. Included in his scribblings were his major taskings, who was doing what, key due dates, and his top priorities for the coming week. He was excellent at planning, coordinating, and executing plans, but also, at holding

people accountable for their deliverables. He continued to extend his track record of success over the years.

- In a few cases, there were these high impact performers who had the respect of others, but people may not have wanted them on their team. They were very good, very sharp, highly productive people but could be demanding, aggressive/assertive, they would rub some people the wrong way, and present management challenges as a result. They didn't have much patience for people who may not pick things up fast enough, or get things done as fast as they might want. It was very beneficial to have learned early in EDS leadership training that "some of your best people will be the hardest to manage." I might have otherwise thought that certain people were not a fit for the organization, but they instead proved time and time again to be the linchpin for project successes. Sometimes, ensuring a project's overall success with such a top performer may come at the expense of having some unhappy teammates and even customers, and the burden will be on you to be more closely engaged to deal with the resulting team dynamic through to project completion. But again, they are high impact producers and critical to your organization.

I highlighted top performers above to help you identify them, but also to make sure you appropriately recognize and reward them. You want to make sure that you keep these people. But remember, the majority of your people are good performers whom you need to value and appreciate as well. Never forget and never take them for granted – good, solid performers are the lifeblood for any successful company.

I, myself, through my career mostly felt that I was a "good" performer, sometimes a very good performer, but also quite a few times an underperformer not pulling my weight – particularly when taking on something new/different and feeling "stupid" again. Rarely did I consider myself a top performer, and never did I consider myself an "exceptional" performer.

Throughout most of my career, whenever I got a promotion or a top assignment, rather than feeling like I really deserved it, I instead just felt grateful, and that I probably squeaked by someone else, or that I was only the best they could find at the time.

The result of my life experience, I'm sure.

How can you improve your performance and value? Ask yourself:

- What have I done to improve service to my customers?
- What have I done recently to increase my value to my team, manager, company?
- What have been my major contributions?
- What impact have I made to my project's success?
- What have I done to go above and beyond what others have done?
- What am I doing to go above and beyond what others are doing?
- What can I do to be more productive in getting needed work done?
- Are there problems or needs that are critical to the project that I could volunteer to tackle that no one else wants?
- What can I do to position myself to have the skills that the company will be needing?

Discretionary Time and Self Investment

What is "discretionary time"? Very simply, it's a block of time where you can freely choose what to do. You've completed your work for the day, you've also done all the things you needed to do at home like the house chores, etc., and you can now do whatever, like watching TV, or reading a book, or enjoying a hobby.

Well, I spent most of my discretionary time on work-related things. But it wasn't like I didn't have anything else to do. I felt like I needed to study and plan, and prepare, and work to keep up with the requirements of my job – just to keep my head above water.

Again, it was mainly driven by a fear of failure and not wanting to embarrass myself or let people down who were depending on me. I used to spend hours of "discretionary time" with my nose to the grindstone learning about microcomputers, programming languages, software tools, etc. But as I moved up the leadership ranks, I thought about things like: what is the purpose of my team or organization, and what's my philosophy of leadership.

I also often gave thought to what to present and say at the next account or all-hands meeting to better inform people, or to provide context on what the organization is going through in the tough competitive climate. Then how could I be a better leader for my team and people? Also, as I pointed out earlier, I always invested in myself to try to be more productive and valuable, and I did not expect the company to pay for everything.

I was always surprised to see people who expected the company to pay for everything that may have increased their productivity or value, above what is normally provided to everyone in the office.

Discretionary time can also be considered as voluntary time, or time you could have used to do something else, but because you want to help out your team or teammate, or because you appreciate being treated well at work, you decide to use this time to give back. It is also time that you choose to use to help people who you feel have helped you. How much discretionary time would you use to support or help someone who never appreciates your work or always takes advantage of you?

If you are a manager or leader who is fair, appreciative, and supportive of your employees, you will likely have people rallying to support you with more of their discretionary time when the need arises.

You would probably offer/exert much less discretionary time, for a manager who is arrogant, demanding, uncaring, and unappreciative.

With that kind of a manager, you probably wouldn't put in that extra effort, or have the desire to be innovative and creative, or give your work that special touch, and instead use your discretionary time elsewhere. That's simply human nature.

Tips for Working with Your Manager – What Your Manager Wants from You

1. Make sure your manager never gets "blindsided."

Among the worst things to happen to a manager is to be blindsided, like being among the last to know about a huge problem in her/his organization. Make sure to give your manager the heads-up of any problem that you may have created, or that has come to your attention – even the hint of a potential problem. It's your responsibility to keep your manager from being caught flat-footed with some big customer problem or organizational issue. The intent is to allow your manager time to get up to speed on the problem, develop solutions, and have a plan of action which he/she can convey to anyone who may be pressing for answers.

> **Example:** Your manager gets a call from your customer saying that he heard from someone on your team that the project deadline was in jeopardy of being missed.
>
> **Scenario 1:** Your manager was blindsided and is forced to say something like: "When did you hear that and would you know from whom? Sorry, but I'll have to investigate further. I'll get back to you asap."
>
> **Scenario 2:** You responsibly gave your manager the heads up, so she's now better prepared: "Yes, sorry I wasn't able to get ahead of this and inform you sooner. I've been gathering information so I could apprise you of the situation. I've identified the source of this concern, and I'm working on adding an additional resource to ensure that we stay on schedule. The pace is picking up on the project so starting tomorrow, I've established daily touch-point meetings to make sure we stay on schedule, to address any issues, and to ensure everyone is on the same page. I'll call you and give you an update tomorrow, close of business your time."

2. Anticipate what your manager needs.

Always try to anticipate what your manager might need. It might be providing an update on some pressing project or issue. Make sure you've done your homework and can be brief and concise.

This is important: think of questions that will likely be asked of you, and either have the answers ready or proactively provide that info as part of your update. Don't pop in all the time and be a nuisance, but if something is on their top 5 list of priorities, updates would probably be appreciated.

Be attentive to how much your updates are being valued to determine how often updates might be needed, or if needed at all. Keep in mind that if the concern is diminishing, it's likely due to your manager's growing confidence with you handling the situation.

You might be thinking, well how many times would make me a nuisance, or how do I know if it's on the top 5. You can start by asking. Or you just have to do it and get a feel for it. You'll figure it out and get good at it.

Just make sure your manager or leader doesn't have to keep asking you for updates.

3. Don't be "high maintenance."

This is similar to the "low maintenance" discussion earlier, but it's worth mentioning again here.

Don't be one who requires high maintenance from your manager.

These are the very few people who frequently seem to be unhappy, dissatisfied with things, like to complain a lot, who seem to enjoy griping with others about how bad things are, or maybe need frequent approval or validation for their work.

If something is negatively impacting the business or the team's productivity, and if it is high on the priority or impact list, then take action to get it addressed.

Don't just grouse about it.

4. Help your manager to be successful.

In my later years with EDS/HP, I had no interest in advancing up the management chain. I was a project manager with more experience and self-confidence, and although my priority was always to do an excellent job, my focus was to ensure that my manager succeeded and "looked good" in the eyes of their managers and peers. I could recall numerous times when I managed large teams, I received acknowledgments for the good and high visibility work done by my people. At this point in my career, I just wanted to give back. I didn't need or want a promotion, and I wasn't looking for more money. I told my then manager straight out that I was there to make the biggest impact that I could, but that I had no interest in moving into higher levels of management.

I told him that my priority and focus was to help him and his organization succeed.

It turned out to be more of a win-win than I had ever anticipated because over the months my manager charged me with more responsibility. I gained more authority and autonomy over a larger group, which was right up my alley anyway, and I unexpectedly received more recognition, verbally and also monetarily, even with the Government Group's ever-present tight budget constraints.

The point is that often, focusing on helping others to succeed, brings you more success as an unintended side effect.

Here's a valuable lesson. In one of the large conference calls that I pulled together, but where this manager was not able to attend, at the start of the meeting there were some humorous comments made about why he couldn't be there, nothing disrespectful or anything mind you, but I kept it very professional, explaining that I didn't know why he couldn't make it but knew that he had several priority matters that he was addressing. I could have easily joined in on the mild humor but stayed 100% committed to supporting him, so I left it at that, and kicked-off the meeting. It turned out that this manager was able to join the call, just a little late, and was listening in.

I was glad that he was able to see/hear that I would demonstrate my support for him whether he was present or not. The point is if you are supporting someone, support that person

100% and 100% of the time. If my manager had heard me laugh along or poke a little fun at his expense even a tiny bit because I wrongly assumed that he was not there, I would have felt lousy about it as soon as I learned that he indeed was on the call. It also might have compromised his trust in me – even a tiny bit.

After this organization was moving along in good order, I was pulled in by another manager to help with his organization, where he asked me to "do what you just did for that organization, but now for my group." An important note: these managers were always supportive and appreciative of my efforts, which was always important to me. I often hear people say that you should do things to help others without the expectation of receiving anything in return. And I agree with that philosophy to a point, where, for example, I've helped people get out of a jam on the highway and would never accept money offered in return.

However, I do think it's important to offer and receive "thank yous." So in all honesty, I probably wouldn't have done as much as I did for these managers if they didn't appreciate my work. So I used more of my discretionary time to support them. And these were simple verbal or email thank yous that I received to express their gratitude for my efforts.

My father always used to tell me, when someone helps you out, always show your appreciation and always reciprocate.

But remember, appreciation goes both ways. You always hear about the need for the manager to show their appreciation to their employees.

As an individual performer, make sure you don't pass up opportunities to thank your manager as well.

5. Be willing to take on tough assignments.

Tell your manager you're willing to take on a difficult and challenging task or project, or one with a tough schedule. Although this was during the latter part of my career, and as a formal project manager, I finally had the self-confidence to tell my manager that I'd be more than willing to take on his most difficult projects, and or, ones with the most difficult customers.

You have to be willing to work extremely hard, be prepared to sacrifice some personal and family time, be ready to make some difficult decisions, and face harsh challenges but someone has to do the job. Your manager won't give you something she/he knows you are not prepared to handle – their credibility is also on the line – but if you get the assignment, in most cases, you immediately get credibility and leverage to get the resources you need, as well as receive the help and guidance that you'll need to make the project a success.

Just make sure you keep your manager apprised of the good and bad, and tap whomever you need for advice or help. When you are a manager faced with a multitude of priority things that need to get done, you will feel extremely fortunate and grateful to have your people pulling together to help, and especially those who step up to take some tough ones off your plate.

6. What if you need to raise concerns?

If you see anything illegal, unethical, or other bad behavior, you need to raise these concerns to your manager promptly. Of course, if it's an urgent personal matter or emergency, bring it up without hesitation.

If your concerns are not in these categories, then assess how it might fit in with the overall challenges your team and organization are facing – in-other-words how important and urgent is your concern.

Give thought to, if your concern were to be addressed and resolved today, what would be the overall benefit to your team or organization, and how might that stack up with the organization's priorities?

Some people don't have a good sense of the overall importance or priority of their concern, nor of the proper timing to bring up their concern.

Never go into your manager's office with a long list, but rather try to narrow your focus to the top two or three concerns. Your manager likely has a number of urgent demands on his/her plate and may not be readily able to pull in people who have extra time to respond to your concerns as fast as you might like.

Always be prepared to explain the problem and clearly describe the negative impact it is having on the team – how this is slowing things down, or causing confusion, or redundant work. Think through and present some alternatives – you being closer to the problem, will hopefully have some suggested solutions. Then step up to help which may require extra work, or even extra-extra work on your part, to help find a fix and implement the needed changes.

7. Don't walk into your manager's office with a major concern and always expect quick action.

Of course, if it's a personal emergency or a critical issue impacting a high visibility customer or project you'll likely get immediate attention. But if it's not, even if it took you a week to prepare and build up the courage to bring up your concern to your manager, have reasonable expectations on how quickly your manager may be able to address your concerns.

Don't expect that your manager will clear off his/her desk and have your problem solved within the hour or by the end of the day. Keep in mind that your manager may have numerous priority issues or deliverables related to a project, or a customer, or owed to her/his management. But you should be given an assurance that he/she will follow up with you, with some estimated time, and you should absolutely get a follow-up.

8. Sometimes it's better to have to apologize rather than to ask for permission.

If you are new to the job, you, of course, need to be very prudent and get the OK to do certain things, but as you gain in experience, your manager will value you more if you can make decisions on your own without always needing permission or validation.

One of Ross Perot's lessons we learned early on was "see snake, kill snake." Sometimes you won't have time to get permission, or pull a committee together, brainstorm alternatives, prioritize, and then finalize a solution.

Another lesson we learned was "Sometimes it's better to ask for forgiveness rather than ask for permission." There will be times where you have to make a decision and take some action

– your best call for the situation, where inaction or a delay to get permission may not be an option.

You may not get every judgment call correct, but you better get most of them right. If not you'll learn quickly and get reeled in by your manager very quickly. Then you ask for forgiveness.

And this does not apply if your instinct is telling you that something doesn't seem right or feels unethical.

What Can You Do If Your Boss Doesn't Appreciate You?

I had to include this topic because it might be a common question for many.

Count your blessings if you have a manager or managers that value and appreciate your work and contributions. However, in my experience, I've come upon some people who are just not the type to express or show appreciation, nor to reward commensurate with people's contributions. Worse yet, if they find that they need to because it's brought to their attention, they come across as insincere in their attempts to show appreciation.

I've found that in most cases, it won't help to try to change your boss' behavior by telling her/him that they don't show enough appreciation.

Now on the flip side, there are those who may not outwardly show very much appreciation in their daily employee interactions, but actually, do appreciate good work, and do take care of their employees, and reward them commensurately.

A word of advice: compare your rewards and benefits with others you know who are in similar positions who work for other companies.

If you feel that you've worked hard, brought good value to your company, and deserve better, then start looking for other opportunities. Make sure you do your homework carefully because the grass always seems greener on the other side.

Generally, larger and/or publicly held companies are more widely scrutinized and have to be much more employee-competitive, so their compensation and benefits packages are more transparent. However, I can't speak to how many other companies out there, especially small companies, treat and reward their employees.

When I think about people who spent 15, 20, 30 or more years with a company, I'm hoping that their company owners/managers took good care of them over those years. I then wonder if those employees could have been far better off working for owners and managers who ran a more efficient business, who were much more appreciative of their employees, and who put in more thought and effort toward how they could better reward and care for their workers over their careers.

So if after some investigating and comparisons, you feel that you are not being rewarded competitively, then keep your options open on other companies. Yes, you could do worse, but you could do better.

Don't be blindly and permanently locked into your current employer.

Then when you become a manager or business owner of your own, make sure that you take good care of your employees by comparing yourself/your company to what other companies are doing for their employees, and I'm not referring to latte machines.

Be a Professional Outside of Work

After transferring to one of my new accounts, I joined the group in one of their after-work activities playing softball.

On one occasion, when we got onto the baseball field to warm up, another team came and said they had signed up for the field for that time slot. One of our guys started arguing with the person and the situation got quite heated, almost to the point of a physical altercation. Now I don't know if the person from the other team had started in a rude or confrontational manner, but we certainly were not innocent of blame in the escalation. We ultimately left, but that was not the end of the story.

The next day, I learned that our account manager received a call from the business owner of the employees from the other softball team, informing her on what happened and the rudeness and verbal altercation that occurred on the field the night before. Our person got a grilling, but we all learned a valuable lesson. Not only was this bad behavior plain and simple, but also, that even though we were not on work time, we were representatives of the EDS account, and that this reflected very badly on the company as well as our account manager. So the account manager required him to go to the other company's place of business, meet with the people with whom he had argued, and personally apologize to them.

I took that to heart and always remembered from that point on that I should always think of myself as a company professional and representative. I don't act a certain way at work, and a different way out in public.

When I see some rude or aggressive behavior by people in public, I often wonder what these people would think if their boss, manager, or company owner found out about his or her bad behavior out in public. How many would reprimand their employee and how many wouldn't care?

It would really get down to the values of the owners and leaders of the company, from the small mom & pop companies to the large multinational corporations.

I also think that those who are aggressive, hostile, belligerent, and rude out in public are doing a huge disservice to themselves and their families because I can't imagine that their attitude would be very different at work. It seems like they would be limiting their financial rewards, advancement, and success in life.

In my experience with EDS, people with even a hint of that type of behavior or attitude would quickly get a warning.

A repeat or any worse behavior and they would very quickly be let go and escorted out of the building.

CHAPTER 2: EXPECT UNCOMFORTABLE, OVERWHELMING, EVEN TERRIFYING SITUATIONS

Don't Quit

In your career progression, starting as an individual performer, you'll very likely find yourself in situations where you are so overwhelmed by what you've been tasked to do, or suddenly realize how "impossible" an assignment has turned out to be, that you might find yourself overcome with fear. You may even break out into a panic or cold sweat, thinking you can't do this and will fail. It's happened to me. Take deep breaths, settle down, take some more deep breaths, calm down and try to relax a little more – and you will calm down eventually – then get back to work and persevere. Ask for assistance and guidance, but don't give up or quit.

Why? Because you'll probably feel really, really lousy about it, and for a long time after you decided to give up. But also, if you stick with it, you will get through it, maybe not even successfully, but either way, you will learn invaluable lessons that you'll be able to carry and apply for your benefit later. If you quit, when you are faced with other very tough challenges in the future, and you no doubt will have more and tougher ones to face, you'll have a greater likelihood of quitting again. So stick with it – you can do it!

And by the way, similarly, do not take a sick day because you feel overwhelmed with the pressures and fear at work. If you are ill and could potentially get others sick, then stay home. But otherwise, get up, go to work, face the music, and work through it. Then take some pride in yourself for pushing through it, even if it turned out to be another bad day. If you don't, and instead take a sick day to avoid problems that will not go away and will only get worse, it too will get easier to do again, and you know you'll only feel worse.

I had been tempted to do just that a number of times, but I ultimately never took a sick day to avoid problems or stresses at work.

Terrified

At my first assignment with EDS, I worked on a Hydro Survey system with the US Army Corps of Engineers at Fort Shafter, Hawaii. This was a computer system that used transponders, fathometers, and a small boat to survey harbor depths around the State to determine how much dredging was needed. As an EDS employee, I was a contractor to the US Army. I was hired to replace someone who was being let go because the project was months behind schedule and the customer was extremely unhappy. There was a week-long overlap so the person I was replacing could bring me up to speed on the project. This could have been extremely uncomfortable, but lucky for me, the person I was replacing was glad to be getting out of there because of the difficult technical requirements, and especially because of the demanding customer. He was very helpful and gracious with his time and treated me really well.

The job required FORTRAN, Enhanced BASIC, and CalComp graphics experience, which I had from my work at the University. In my second week on the job, I remember like it was yesterday, sitting at my desk reviewing thousands of lines of code, suddenly feeling a rush, my face getting flushed, getting cold sweat, heart pounding, and experiencing sheer panic, thinking, how did I get myself into this situation – this is way over my head, I'm not smart enough for this, and I'm going to fail. This was only weeks into this new job. My mind was racing – I have a wife and young son, and a new house with a mortgage – what am I going to do? I somehow settled down, got my nose back to the grindstone, put in some hard work, started to make some progress, and months later succeeded in fixing the problems and enhancing the overall system, ultimately receiving praise from the customer who was the chief of that engineering branch.

As I learned over time, me being "stupid" again, meaning that I'm in a new job where I'm basically clueless, was to happen many more times, and was just a normal part of career advancement. You always have to take on big challenges to stretch, improve, and increase your value. Your worth, and part of every job is not only what you can do well, but how well you can pick up new, unfamiliar work, and how well you can handle the stress, discomfort, and criticism of being/feeling "stupid," as you pick things up. Be aware and accept as part of the package that people may criticize you and even ask "why are you here?" And yup, I've gotten that! The more you can take on these challenges, persevere and succeed, the more valuable you become to the team, your manager, and the company in the long run. Also, understand that these challenges won't always turn out to be successes.

As my career progressed and I gained more experience and confidence, it became kind of a "badge of honor" to get thrown in to take on new and difficult challenges, and to become "stupid" again, knowing I would figure it out. Sometimes the work needed to get done, and there simply wasn't anyone else who could or would do it. Maybe I wouldn't be great, but I'd at least be good enough to get the job done.

I also used to be terrified just thinking about a scheduled meeting where I had to give a presentation. I was afraid and nervous about giving presentations every single time. Shaking hands, voice quivering – I came to realize that I was wired that way because it didn't matter how much I prepared and how many times I would practice. I was always envious of others who were "naturals" at giving presentations, and others who say they were so nervous but when they were up giving their presentation, they appeared fine. For me, it was always a frightful experience. Because my hands would shake I always wanted to have a podium so I could rest my notes on it, or have PowerPoint slides up, and I never held a piece of paper in my hands to read off, or it would be shaking like a leaf. I also learned not to pick up a glass of water when giving a presentation because that turned out awful once. A quick sip of bottled water worked much better.

The point I'm making is that advancing in your career will require you to get up in front of audiences, maybe it's only your team at first, but eventually much larger groups, but you don't always have to be smooth, relaxed, and polished with public speaking. I am proof of that. Of primary importance is that you have important information to share, and you prepare your message well. You'll find out very quickly if you're the type who can do very well just winging it, or if this doesn't work for you at all. If winging it doesn't, then never give a presentation underprepared. Don't be fooled by what you see in the movies about people being able to stand up, throw away their prepared notes, and from the sheer importance of the moment, eloquently convey their message with the audience being inspired and in awe. I've seen some people being interviewed on TV with a heartfelt message to send and thinking that their emotion and sincerity will carry the day, who ultimately bungle the job. They come off emotional, but with no coherent message.

For some people, like me, that won't happen without preparation. Take the time to write down what you want and need to say, like your top 3 to 5 critical points, then review them, then re-review them to make sure you are concise and will be understood by your audience. Make sure you're not giving muddled information, or you'll miss a golden opportunity to get out an important message.

Again, write it down, review it, and practice – not necessarily to be polished, although it will help, but primarily to get your most critical and meaningful points out there and understood.

As much as possible, don't use it as a crutch, but if you absolutely need to, refer to your notes to make sure you cover what you wanted – I've done this many times. It's more important to get your message out rather than to satisfy critics who say that you should never read from your notes.

Over time, this preparation will take less and less time, and you'll get better and better at it, even if you're still nervous when presenting it.

Another thing I once learned about giving presentations from an EDS class, to make sure your audience gets your message: "first, tell 'em what you're gonna tell 'em, tell 'em, then tell 'em what you just told 'em."

Uncomfortable

1. Why are you here?

Back at Fort Shafter, because of the work I did with the Corps of Engineers, I was asked to move to the Management Information Systems Office (MISO) to start a new EDS team. My first assignment there was to support a new effort to start interfacing PCs with their IBM mainframe working under their tech lead, a Sergeant. I quickly got the vibe that he didn't like "contractors," and when he learned I had not worked with an "IRMA" card before which back then was one of the first interfaces connecting PCs to mainframe computers, he pretty much had a fit and told me straight out "why are you here?" He complained to his management and my manager that I was not qualified for the job. The next day, he came to my work area, unplugged the IBM PC that was assigned to me, one of only a few on the entire base at the time, and without a word, walked out the door with it. He obviously felt that I was not worthy of having it, but it was my primary tool to satisfy the contract requirements.

It took a week of back and forth with the higher-ups at that office, the government contracting office, and EDS, but the Sergeant's actions were eventually countermanded. One morning he walked back in carrying the PC equipment, personally hooked everything back up and made sure it was functional, then walked back out, again, without saying a word the entire time. He could easily have sent someone else to return it, but he chose to suck it up and do it himself, and I admired him for that. He was never friendly toward me, but we did communicate, minimally and professionally.

I eventually learned this entirely new IBM Disk Operating System (DOS) and applications like Lotus 1-2-3 on my own and applied it directly to what I was doing. I put on demonstration classes so the customer could become familiarized with the functionality of Personal Computers, PC based spreadsheets (Lotus), word processing (WordPerfect), and databases or filing systems (dBase). As it turned out this expanded into other PC work, it made the customer and my manager quite happy, and it actually led to the customer increasing the team size, and therefore revenue for EDS. It went from just myself to 10 people. I still remember receiving a letter of recognition from our Division Manager who was in San Diego, saying that I increased the EDS team "10 fold". It meant a lot to me that an EDS Manager from the "mainland," took the time to write and send me this letter of recognition and thank you.

2. Some people simply won't like you.

Be prepared to find that some people will just not like you, or are uncomfortable with you for whatever reason. For me, the few that I can recall were never poor performers but were instead good performers.

There seems to be a lack of chemistry sometimes, and other times I think some people may be suspicious of your intentions, simply because of your position and their life experience. These were few and far between, but it was obvious when I got bad or odd vibes from some people, and they didn't respond to my attempts to be friendly towards them.

From my experience, my advice would be to not spend/waste time trying to figure out why. Treat them as you do with everyone else, giving no special attention, and focus on the rest of your team and how you can best work with and support them.

It's also important to distinguish these people from those who may be a little intimidated by you because of your experience or leadership position. They are usually more afraid that they are maybe not on par, or not measuring up to your expectations. As opposed to the other people who may not like you, these people generally respond very positively to your friendliness and appreciate your out-reach to them.

3. I didn't want the promotion.

When my former manager, who was the Account Manager of the Systems Engineering Center, asked me to be his back-up, I was a little uncomfortable about it. That's a big deal because in any number of situations, you become the decision-maker. Then about a year later, he asked me to be his replacement. I told him then that I was really uncomfortable with the promotion offer. I indicated that I didn't think that I was qualified to do the job. I asked multiple times why not this other manager, a peer, who I thought was better qualified. I felt that I didn't have the needed experience, nor qualities, nor that "executive presence" to be at that level of management.

However he insisted that he had confidence in me, and persisted, and I reluctantly relented to take the opportunity and promotion. And I have been forever glad that I did.

So I accepted the position and embraced the job, but again, a big reason was that I did not want to disappoint the person who took the risk to recommend me to his management and getting the approval. I stayed on in this role for seven years, and the organization eventually expanded from about 75 to 192 people, with ten managers reporting to me.

The lesson here is that you can't always go on your "gut" or instinct. My gut, my intuition, and every fiber in my body told me that I was not cut out for this.

If you are presented with opportunities, especially if someone you trust insists that you can do it, then grab it, work hard and do your best. You sometimes have to push through these feelings, as well as deep fears, and be willing to take huge risks to advance in your career.

If it turns out that you miss the mark or even fail, then make that an opportunity to learn and improve – never wallow in "I shouldn't have."

Humbled and Demoralized, the Low Point in My Career – My Stint in Sales

Although I spent many years in management with EDS, I had taken only one formal business class which was Econ101: Microeconomics, which I had taken as an evening class before I started with EDS. I always wanted a stronger business background and to ultimately earn an MBA. I actually went through the entire admissions process at the University of Hawaii in 1985, got accepted, purchased all my books for the first semester, then EDS lost the re-bid for the government contract. I then dropped out of the MBA program to move to the mainland to stay with EDS.

After finally getting an MBA in 1999, I started looking for new opportunities in EDS. I had been with the Systems Engineering Centers for about 15 years and was the Southern California SE Center manager for seven years, so I wanted to find a new challenge with the company. I remembered hearing from one top company executive years earlier, that to advance in a company, you need to "punch your time" in Sales. I thought this would be a perfect way to leverage a freshly minted MBA, and also thought that this could be lucrative because I consistently put in long hours, with evenings and weekend work, and felt that Sales rewarded people more commensurately with long hours on sales deals.

I knew that this would be a huge uphill climb, not having any prior sales experience, nor deep IT hardware/software/outsourcing experience which is what we were selling, but I figured that I had always overcome major learning curves before and felt that it was a reasonable risk to take. After transferring into the EDS Sales Organization, as a Business Development, Sales Support person, it turned out to be the worst two years of my career in EDS. I don't regret having made the move into sales because the experience was extremely enlightening and valuable, but it was clearly not my cup of tea.

When joining the sales group, I learned this phrase: "Nothing happens until someone sells something!" I found this to be eye-opening and illuminating. Through my business coursework, I had studied Sales and Marketing in fairly great depth, but this brought it all home in a clear and concise manner. That simple phrase was like seeing a complex process in physics being boiled down to an elegant equation. EDS, this large multinational information technology corporation, with over 130,000 employees at the time in 2000, started with Ross Perot selling one piece of business to one customer in 1962. To sustain and continue to grow the company, people had to keep selling EDS business ever since, or not much else would have happened.

I was in way over my head, again. Being in some of the sales meetings was extremely different for me and way technical as solutions to customer needs were being architected. It was at times like sitting in a room with French speakers. "Hey, you were at the meeting right?" Yup, sat through the whole thing – didn't understand a word.

Here's one of the emails I sent to a friend and fellow MBA student in September 2000: "Hey Bob! Now I'm in these Sales meetings, and I swear, it's like I'm on Mars - they're using a language, words, strategies, pricing scenarios, etc. that are totally foreign to me! It's sure stressful not knowing much of what's going on and not feeling I'm contributing much, but I'm getting a real charge knowing I'm learning a whole new side of the business. It's exciting alright!"

The culture was also very different than what I was used to with my EDS experience up to that point. On the first day at the sales office which was in Costa Mesa, I remember walking to my desk and commenting that this Costa Mesa office was very nice, and one of the more experienced sales support persons there responded in all seriousness, "in this neck of the woods, we say "Coast-a Mesa, not Cost-a Mesa." Hmm, Ok... My wife speaks some Spanish so I had to go home to confirm how it was pronounced. Later I thought, back in Hawaii, if you were new to the islands and said "hew-mu-nu-ku-akapaka" no one would tell you, "brah, that's our state fish, and around here we say humuhumunukunukuapua'a." Anyway, that was my first day in sales.

In every other part of the company that I had been, co-workers, peers, your managers, everyone kind of helped each other out – encouraged you if you're down, try to down-play a mistake, and never throw you under the bus. In Sales, my immediate co-workers definitely went over and above to help me out whenever I needed it. They were my life-line, and I was grateful to them. But as an organization, it was very high stress and highly competitive, and you're pretty much on your own if you screw up. I heard the term "falling on your sword" quite a bit, and it sure felt that way at times where you could go down in flames. It's very hard to describe because it was so different from any other work environment I had experienced. Now I never saw anything underhanded or unethical or anything like that. But the overall feeling was very different – I guess it was more of a dog-eat-dog environment. I remember it being so stressful going into the office sometimes, that on some days, with an almost one hour commute on the 405, I was glad it was taking so long and actually hoped for heavier traffic so it would take longer.

In Sales, I got to see an entirely different side of this very large company. Compared to what I had experienced before, the expense accounts in the sales group were unbelievable with spending for travel, wining and dining of customers and potential customers, lavish corporate sales events, large bonuses, etc. Everything I had experienced in EDS before sales, and after sales, was with tight and heavily scrutinized budgets and expenses, and very limited spending.

I actually did fine compensation wise as I supported Sales Executives working on proposals for Boeing, Mattel, Red Bull, Avery Dennison, and The Getty Museum among others. There were some components of sales support in which I could do OK, like arranging for the solutions and engineering folks to come together, pulling together the initial financials for the proposals, coordinating the meetings with the customers, and preparing the presentation and proposal materials for the meetings. Of the prospects I worked on, we did sign several which totaled about $20 million in sales, although none were new logos. This is definitely not to brag because for many colleagues this was a small amount, but it's to provide some context.

But there were other aspects where I was less than satisfactory. Here are some of them:
- Although I got positive reviews from the sales executives that I supported and from those who were directly training and supporting me, I did not get positive reviews from everyone who provided input, including my direct

manager and a manager who was at the regional headquarters.

- The input I received was that I was not enough of a take-charge person in meetings, to drive toward customer solutions. From my perspective, I was totally out of my element. I couldn't drive towards solutions because this was in large part, a highly technical world, with hardware, computing, networking, integration, data center consolidations, service contracts, and other IT solutions that were way out of my experience base. Although I started out with EDS in the technical arena, most of my experience was now in organizational management, budgeting/expense tracking, and compensation management, among other things. Trying to come up to speed in the sales support arena was like "drinking out of a fire hose," but I had faced and overcome such challenges before. In this case, however, time was not on my side when multimillion-dollar sales deals, people's large commissions, and individual and regional sales quota numbers are being acutely scrutinized. Add to that the fact that competitors were constantly and intensely eyeing for any sliver of an opportunity to rip customers away from us. Losing to competitors after tons of work and expenses to fly in experts, design solutions, develop the pricing, and pull together the proposals was devastating, and where heads could roll as a result.

- On one occasion, I pushed back on some work so I would have more time on an assignment. I can't ever recall another instance where I pushed back, but I was struggling to keep my head above water and didn't want to screw things up for the sales executive that I was supporting. My action ultimately led to a perception that I was unwilling to accept additional work, and for some reason, that I resented reporting to, and taking orders from a person who was younger than me. To not respect a manager of mine would be totally out of character for me, and I had worked for another manager who was younger than me for many years at EDS and who happened to be a female. This age thing became a very big deal as it turned out. This disrespect concern, with my push-back issue, and my not being able to take charge was escalated to upper management, giving me the kind of visibility you never want – the negative kind.

- But I was also not really a good personality fit for the sales organization. I was never the extrovert and never comfortable in a room full of people that I didn't know, especially salespeople where, let's be honest, image and self-confidence-wise, I was not in the same league with these folks. I also never had the gift of gab to comfortably chat with folks about sports or politics or anything for that matter. I was always low-key by nature but would be perfectly comfortable conversing more on a personal level in a setting with a few people.

The actual confirmation that I wasn't doing well occurred one day when my immediate manager wouldn't even make eye contact with me when talking to myself and two other co-workers, standing around during a meeting break. And ten times worse when I traveled to the Regional Sales office in the Bay Area and a higher level manager passes me by in a long narrow hallway and doesn't even acknowledge my presence. At first, I came up with all these reasons why he didn't recognize me, but it was simply denial. He had taken me out on a couple of sales calls, so he knew who I was. I realized then that from management's view, I was a big transfer mistake. It was pretty demoralizing. During this low point, quitting might have entered my mind, but I never gave it serious consideration. I was hoping that over the next year I would gain enough experience to put myself on a solid footing, if I survived that long.

So my reputation in sales was less than positive, to put it mildly, but I still give tremendous credit to those folks in sales. It is a fast-paced, high pressure, sink or swim, feast or famine, and a no mercy environment in which to survive. My two years with them definitely made me wiser, and a more well-rounded EDS career person. Another bright spot was the support I received from the regional sales manager who headed the Costa Mesa office. We had known each other for years and were both USC grads. He used to lease space from us at the SE center, and I could never beat him at ping pong, although they were close games.

When the Sales group had a large corporate-wide layoff, my immediate manager in Costa Mesa, who had that age difference concern, was key to my getting my next opportunity with EDS' Government Services Group. He hustled to put things into place to make the transfer happen. He did not have to do that, so I was fortunate and grateful for his efforts.

This experience represented the absolute low point in my career with EDS. But here again, reflecting on EDS Leadership training from many years earlier helped me a great deal. It was emphasized to us that in your EDS career progression, "failure may be OK." We learned that employees could have failures that do not define their overall and long-term value to the company.

I don't remember the exact scenarios, but I do remember training videos that showed a number of examples of employees who failed in one area, but when given the opportunity, excelled in other areas of the company – the lesson for managers and decision makers being, to not immediately give up on an employee if they failed at something. I had never experienced failure in my job but had enough successes and confidence to know that I could overcome this and do well again somewhere else in EDS. With the layoffs in sales, I transferred to Government Services and had another 12 successful years with the company. And I didn't hide out in a dark cubicle in some forgotten corner of the company being complacent and collecting a paycheck until retirement.

I thoroughly enjoyed my work after sales, and I continued to receive new and challenging opportunities, traveled across the country, received very good reviews, promotions, bonuses, stock options, and earned professional credentials including PMI's PMP for project management.

This shows that one can come back very successfully from a career low point, as long as you continue to work hard and strive to bring value to your customer, co-workers, your manager, and your company.

Balancing Work and Personal Time Can be Difficult

One of my long-time colleague and friend was an excellent example of someone who reflected solid commitment to his work but maintaining balance with his family. He consistently showed me that you don't need to kill yourself at work to be successful. I always admired him for his disciplined balance of work and family. He was always spot on with his commitments, he would work extra hours whenever it was needed, he was always well prepared for whatever needed to get done, but he was also consistent with his start and end times because of his family commitments, which included supporting his son's baseball activities. He would also proactively schedule meetings with me to keep me apprised of his areas of responsibility, or issues he was running to the ground, so I never had to ask.

That being said, you will inevitably be in situations where you might feel that you could lose the confidence, trust, and respect from your peers, teammates, and manager due to your choices related to project demands. You'll be faced with situations where you'll need to choose work, over something very important to your family or one of your family members. Your family depends on you financially, as with your spouse if they are working. Sacrificing family for work, or vice versa could make the difference on whether you are among the top-ranked employees on your team, or in the middle. I've never seen anyone move to the bottom of the rankings because of their family or other personal commitments.

But even more importantly, your choices over work vs. your personal/family obligations can impact how your co-workers perceive you and your value to the team. It can be personally and emotionally devastating to be the person who didn't come through, or who didn't show up when everyone else did, in a critical part of a project. I'm pointing this out not to criticize those who choose family over work, but to highlight the sacrifice they are making from the work perspective. I've seen the impact on some who chose family over work in critical project times, where they were terribly conflicted and felt extremely guilty, and for a long time after, for not being there to support their teammates. You usually only hear about the negative impact on the person from their family side when a person chooses work over family.

In the case where a project deadline takes priority, you may need to do a better job to explain to your family why you made that choice. They couldn't otherwise understand how torn you could be, and how desperately important it is that in critical project situations, you need to be in the trenches, elbow-to-elbow with your co-workers, and how terrible it can be to disappoint your co-workers and managers if you are not there with them at a critical time. Your ability to provide for your family, and your ability to enhance what you can provide, could be a function of how many family sacrifices you are willing or able to make. But from my experience, employees choosing family over work demands is common, and they still have a track record of solid performance. It should be understood as well, that there will be others who will put in the longer hours, who will likely be contributing more in the project effort, and will, therefore, receive greater rewards and recognition, and will be afforded more opportunities. This simply reflects a typical employee-base and project team.

In the early days with EDS, we had many "death marches" where we worked 12 to 14 hours or more per day, seven days per week, with some all-nighters, and this would be for weeks and even months at a time. We lost many good people as a result. These incredible and unreasonable project demands diminished dramatically over time, but things like this can happen, so be prepared to make some difficult work vs. family choices.

CHAPTER 3:
SO YOU WANT TO BE A MANAGER?

Context

In this chapter I discuss some of the important facets of being a manager, to help you make a more informed decision on whether you should pursue this path. I examine some of the difficult aspects with which I had to cope and overcome as a manager.

Growing up, I always tried to be the nice, friendly guy to others. I'm sure that because of my disappointments and shortcomings as I mentioned earlier, I may have overcompensated and as a result always wanted people to like me.

Because of these life experiences, I've developed a strong empathy for people, I prefer that people feel welcomed and comfortable, and I never wanted to upset anyone. Unless, of course, I'm being poorly treated, for whatever reason. However, as a supervisor or manager, you have to get over wanting everyone to like you.

You can't be everyone's friend all the time.

This certainly doesn't mean that you have to become an SOB, but it does mean that you have to learn to sometimes put your business, project, team, or customer priorities, ahead of what a team member or team may want. You'll have to get over being worried about what people will, or are, thinking about you and your decisions. I had no problem confronting people if they were being rude, or arrogant, or grossly unfair, but this was very uncommon in my experience with EDS.

It's much more difficult having to bring up unpleasant things to people who are working hard and doing their best but may not be meeting expectations.

Although I was rascal and always in trouble as a kid, I became the "quiet one" as I got older, especially at work, in meetings, and in classes. People generally had to ask me for input or I wouldn't say anything for fear of looking stupid. I had to consciously and consistently work on building up my courage to take risks and speak up as I became a member of a leadership team. There were times when I maybe didn't have the smartest thing to say, but there were more times when I started to find that "hey, I think I provided some good input." Even after saying something "stupid" and feeling embarrassed and self-conscious, I learned that I could get over it, and it would bother me less because I was enjoying the satisfaction of providing input that was actually providing benefit to the team or my manager.

As I've found, for some people it is not a huge deal to bring matters up that may upset people. Then, of course, there are others who simply don't care what other people think of them, but I found these latter folks to be rare in my time with EDS. For me, my concern as to how people viewed me was one of my biggest hurdles to overcome, and it took years to gain the experience and confidence to be able to make decisions and calls that would upset or disappoint people, and not have it seriously bother me.

So to emphasize, if you want to be a manager, you have to be able to cope with people being upset with you or maybe even not like you, because of the decisions you sometimes have to make for the greater good of the team, the customer, the organization, or the company.

Another aspect of being a manager that I had to let go was providing employees with assurances that strong performance will always lead to opportunities and compensation growth, and also conveying a sense of security that everyone will have long careers with the company, commensurate with their contributions. The company always seemed to have a bright future, with limitless growth potential, and with many and wide-ranging opportunities, globally. This changed dramatically as industry, and global competition grew, and as cost-cutting became prevalent. This led to hiring freezes, compensation slowdowns and freezes, and ultimately large and sustained layoffs.

Managing in this environment was extremely challenging. We went from being able to reward contributions and good performance with perks, bonuses, and salary increases, to people having to accept that their reward was now down to "thank yous" and pats-on-the-back, and hopefully not getting laid off. Times would then improve, but then get bad again, and these ups and downs continued through to my retirement. As a manager, I found that there are many satisfying and extremely rewarding aspects. But among the downsides: I had to present very unpleasant news to individuals and teams, and manage through times of very low morale because of actions I needed to take.

You already know that the management route is not going to be easy. In this chapter, I hope to provide you with greater insight as to the challenges you'll face as a manager, and some practical advice. In the book, I cover many of the upsides as well.

Your Job as a Manager – Key Success Factors for Leadership and Management

1. **If your main concern is for people to always "like" you, then you will never be a respected and successful leader.**

When people are not performing satisfactorily, when they are behaving in a manner that does not meet your or the company's standards, you must have the courage to confront people one-on-one to make sure they understand from you directly, that they are not meeting your expectations – that their performance needs to improve, or a certain behavior needs to stop.

If you don't take any action, or send someone else to do it, you will undermine and diminish people's respect for you.

If you avoid addressing the issue completely, you'll be allowing and possibly encouraging this level of performance or type of behavior. You'll get what you tolerate – which was another lesson from early EDS leadership training.

When addressing poor performance or behavior, however, never go in upset with guns blazing. Seek first to understand as there may be some underlying explanation or the information you received may have been a biased view, whether intentional or not.

You would never look in only one direction before crossing the street with your children correct? There could be regretful consequences if you do – even on a one-way street where it's so obvious from which direction cars will be coming. I assure you, there will be situations where you'll be glad that you did not jump to a premature conclusion. Then when handling the issue, if coaching is required, always address the specific performance or behavior, not the person.

For example, if you say "you are so cynical" vs. "you behaved or acted in a cynical manner." Or "you are an underperformer" vs. "your performance on this task was not up to par."

2. Demanding and ungrateful.

On the other end of the spectrum, if you are a demanding and ungrateful manager, you may get good short-term results, but in the long-run, you'll most likely only gain basic compliance – and it will be primarily out of fear or avoidance – in-other-words, "we better just shut up and do what he/she says". You may not always get the very best work that people can provide. You'll likely lose people's "discretionary time" as well as their creativity and innovation. Long term, you'll probably not get the voluntary, motivated, and inspired "extra effort" to achieve exceptional results from your employees. You'll also lose good people.

You'll have much greater success at getting the best from your people when you have high expectations, when you hold them accountable for their actions and performance, when you appropriately recognize and reward them, when you are fair and equitable, when you care, and when you behave ethically.

3. You need to consistently hold people accountable for their commitments and deadlines.

I always started with the assumption to trust that people will keep to their commitments, and by far this held true. However, I did learn some hard lessons. To foster an environment where people always keep to their commitments and deadlines, you need to be ready to have some difficult discussions with some people. See more in the next section on "Responsibility and Accountability."

4. As a leader, don't easily give up on people if they decline your offer for an opportunity due to their lack of self-confidence.

You will have an opportunity to play a big part in putting your people on the path of greater achievements, success, and advancement in the company. As you've read, if some of the important people in my past had allowed me to decline opportunities, because of my lack of self-confidence, rather than persisting and encouraging and supporting me, I would not have reached the level of success that I did in my career.

Be a mentor to the younger/newer/less experienced people who are working hard to do a good job, and encourage them to stretch. You could provide them with the launching pad to really spread their wings, and be the catalyst for them to accomplish things way beyond their expectations.

Even if they fall short or even fail at first, your support and encouragement will allow this to be a valuable learning experience and be just a blip in their long and successful career.

5. Never overlook or pass up an opportunity to pat people on the back for their good work, and as importantly for good behaviors.

As a leader, you should acknowledge your people when deserved in your day-to-day interactions with them, not once a month, or during a six-month or annual review. You should seek out and always give credit where credit is due, never take credit when it belongs elsewhere, and never take credit alone for something you should be sharing with others.

6. As a manager, can you be friends with your employees?

In my experience, you definitely can be friends with your employees, and in my opinion, always should. It's much more satisfying and fulfilling at work to have friendships and a friendly work environment. I've also found that in most cases, employees will understand that having a good relationship with your manager does not mean that you will be shielded from sometimes getting "bad news" or reprimands or undesirable assignments.

They'll come to understand that the business or the project has to have over-arching priority over individuals and that every employee really depends upon the success of the team and business for their own livelihood. And as well, there will also be times where you'll have opportunities to go over and above to help your people in times of personal distress or family needs. I was a recipient of this type of caring and compassion a number of times from my managers – managers that I was extremely fortunate to have, and with whom I considered good friends.

7. Make sure you know who your top people are – sometimes you have to seek them out.

I would not have known how good, sharp, fast, and productive some of our SEs were if I had not worked a grueling project with them once. On one of my projects as a relatively new SE Supervisor, I had to lead a team of highly technical "C" programmers on a high visibility and time-sensitive project. It was our first ever effort in the late 1980s to place a General Electric (GE) jet engine hard copy service manual with all the parts and diagrams onto a CD ROM for fast reference and access by aircraft mechanics. I couldn't program a lick in "C," but I was there every hour that they were there, doing anything and everything that I could to help, like with the documentation.

The most demanding part took extremely long hours and weekend work for about two months and included a number of all-nighters.

The point is that I got to see first-hand the skill and productivity of some of our top technical people, working in sustained grueling conditions. And it wasn't only their skill at programming. It was also the speed at which they could type and edit. It was mesmerizing to see them exhausted but still so focused, with the ability to get the ideas from their heads into functional code with consistent lightning speed – typing, selecting, deleting, copying and pasting, cutting and pasting, all with control keys and far faster than with a mouse – real old days key pounding. And to a person, they had great positive, can-do, what-else-can-I-do attitudes, and were a pleasure to work within such high-pressure conditions.

As a manager/leader, it'll be very important to recognize when you have highly productive people, and to value, appreciate, and make sure you keep them.

You may not notice or be aware of them if you only sit in your cube or office. You have to seek them out sometimes, and you can start by asking around.

8. Making people and their families feel comfortable at office gatherings/parties.

As a manager at company gatherings, I never only sat with my family and the group at my table. I would always get up and walk around to meet and chat with employees and their spouses, so they all felt as welcomed and as comfortable as possible. I did get more comfortable with this, but it was not always easy because I was not the extrovert social butterfly type at all. I felt that it was a small but important gesture to show the employees and their families that I valued and appreciated them.

One year, I was even the 5 foot 2, Santa Clause for the employees' children at the company Christmas party, with my 6' 3" tall manager as my elf assistant in his green elf suit. It was hilarious because everyone knew we were going to play Santa and his elf that year, and we were such a contrast in height that it was obvious who was going to be the little elf. There were well over 100 adults and children, and the place erupted with shock and laughter when I came out as Santa with big "Ho Ho Ho's," and with a 6' plus green elf prancing about behind me and showering the children with candy.

This by-the-way was a wonderful experience – to see the smiles, excitement, and gleam in the eyes of all the kids as they were thrilled to see and interact with Santa. My worries about the kids thinking that I would be too short to be a real Santa evaporated in a few seconds – they didn't even notice and couldn't have cared less. Also, right up to the event, I kept trying to get my manager to wear the matching green stretch tights, but he wasn't having any of it.

We had numerous stomach busting laughs on that. He would insist, "No, no, no, that is not happening!"

9. Sometimes you'll have to "embrace" things you think you could never support.

I was at a meeting at Corporate in Plano, Texas once and was listening to Todd Carlson, who was the Chief Information Officer (CIO) at the time, and one of the things he said had a huge impact on me and stayed with me for the rest of my career. He was talking about the many changes going on within EDS and that there were changes that we needed to make that might be extremely uncomfortable, or that we absolutely may not like – "paradigm shift" was commonly heard at the time. He impressed upon everyone that sometimes we had to not only "accept" the changes to move forward, but we had to "embrace" the changes.

That was like a key to a door that I hadn't realized existed before. It was like a light switch got flipped. It presented a path to a complete mindset change from "I don't like this, and it would never work" to, "OK, the play is called, and I'm going to let go of all my negativity on this. I need to support it, do everything I can to make this work, and make sure that it benefits the team and the organization". I believe that this helped to take me up a notch in my ability to increase my value to my leadership team and the company.

Be aware that some people will simply refuse to accept changes. They will bad-mouth, fight, and undermine what they don't like instead. You'll need to identify the last hold-outs and try to change their attitude (good luck). If they impede progress and become a problem in the workplace, you'll need to root them out.

10. A quick tip on delegating or assigning work.

You will have to get comfortable with and very good at delegating work and assignments to others. For some people, you may need to be prepared to get push-back at times. Your response on a tasking may not always be "yes ma'am/sir, how fast did you need this?"

Sometimes for quick taskings, it may be faster to say, in a calm but confident voice, "I need you to…" and present your assignment, as opposed to "could you," or even "I'd like you to." I picked this up from an experienced leader and found that it is not brash or rude, but more definitive, and tends to eliminate having to discuss the options. If you say "could you," or "I'd like you to" it sometimes tends to take more time.

You might get questions on why, or on the pros and cons, or whether the person would like or had time to take the assignment or not. When you instead say something like, "I need you to set things up for an all-hands meeting tomorrow please," it tends to accentuate a sense of urgency, indicates that it's not optional, so you can get down to business on what needs to be done.

But also, if it's a little more involved, you should always explain why this task is important to you. It gives more meaning to the task, and instead of only working on it with blinders, they have a better perspective and vision of what needs to get done, its value, and possibly how better to accomplish the task.

At times, people may be reluctant to bring concerns up to you because they might fear that you will ask them to fix the problem when they're already up to their ears in work. One of the senior technical leads once told me, simple, assign it to someone else to fix. When someone else brings up another problem that needs to be addressed, assign it to another person.

Now obviously you have to be prudent on how and how often you do this, but it's just another tool for your toolbox for an appropriate time, which should actually be rare.

11. Getting serious push-back when assigning work.

You need to be fair and balanced when assigning work. You'll have people who are always willing to take on work, or always agreeable, or at least show that they are. Then you'll also have people who are not so willing, or show some displeasure, or even give you push-back on certain assignments or type of work they basically don't like to do.

When important but less desirable work needs to get done, do you avoid assigning work to some people primarily because you want to avoid their push-back or even a confrontation? To be a respected leader, and to do what's best and fair for your team, you need to step up and do what you know needs to be done. People notice – they can see what's going on and word gets around.

> *Once, several months after I had transferred to SoCal as an SE supervisor, I had a situation like this where I had to ask an experienced SE to take on a TDY assignment that was clearly undesirable. This person initially expressed her reluctance to take on the assignment, so I tried to explain why it was important and why her skills made her the right candidate for this, but she continued to push back on it.*
>
> *I asked if there was any personal situation to consider, but her unwillingness came with no explanation or reason. It was clear that she simply didn't want to do it. I finally said, "so you are refusing the assignment?" It seemed to me that this person had been successful at avoiding assignments she didn't like in the past. She clearly wasn't happy but finally relented and accepted the assignment.*
>
> *She understood that if I had to go back and ultimately explain to the account manager that she had refused an assignment with no justification, it could cause some very negative consequences.*

12. Don't ever think that answers will be obvious and that your decisions will be easy – you may only have bad choices.

You will likely find that many times, instead of having to decide between a bad choice and an obviously good one, you have to decide which bad choice you are willing to live with – and you will not have the option to not choose. In my early EDS training, we learned "you will have to decide which problem you want to live with." In-other-words, you have no good options – only bad ones, so you'll have to decide which is the least bad option.

You'll have to choose one, knowing you'll face the wrath from someone or a group of people because of that choice. It could be from your team, your organization, your customer, or even your manager, so you better have well-thought-out and prepared reasons as to why you made your choice. Now it might be hard to imagine making a choice that you know would upset your customer – the customer is always right, correct?

But here's an example: your project requirements specified by the customer is to provide 5 specific functions. The project has been planned, resourced with a team, costed with a completion deadline, signed, and you are now three quarters through the project. Your customer then realizes that they actually need 7 functions instead of 5, which would take an additional 1 to 2 weeks to complete.

After an analysis, you explain to the customer that you can complete what they need but the deadline will have to be extended, and the cost will have to increase. Most customers will understand, there may be some negotiations, but not a huge problem to resolve. Other customers might be furious because they absolutely need the final product with all 7 functions within the original time-frame and their funding is already maxed. Maybe you choose to go along.

You decide to do the added work and eat the cost to keep your customer happy - which then upsets your team and your manager, especially if they weren't first consulted.

But what if this is the 2nd or 3rd time your customer makes such a demand? So in that case, you might inform your customer that you have to decline the work with the added requirements and need to stay with the originally agreed upon requirements/timeframe/cost, and you now have a very unhappy customer and situation to deal with.

And your manager is still mad at you.

Obvious good/easy choices can be rare sometimes. You may be conflicted with a number of your decisions, but you make a decision and learn to move on.

13. Leverage your key people when making decisions.

When faced with problems and have to make difficult decisions, always try to get input from your key people. You'll get perspectives and possible solutions that had never occurred to you. There have been times when a solution to a problem that impacted the account was so obvious, and I was certain that there couldn't be any dissenters, but where it turned out that I was wrong.

What has saved me from making a poor decision, and instead allowed me to make a much better decision, was getting input from my key people. This, of course, works best when you provide a safe, non-critical environment. People should be open to discuss, be bluntly honest on their opinions, but as importantly, when you make a decision, everyone needs to get on board to support it. This is also how you avoid making one man or one women decisions, and no one knows where the heck that came from.

By getting input and hashing it out, you build core awareness and support for your decisions as well. When your manager makes decisions that you may not initially agree with or support, don't go along reluctantly, dragging your feet. Everyone needs to be fully on board, and with a consistent message going forward. This would not be the case for decisions that are unethical or unfair, and those that may be blatantly and obviously bad decisions. If that's the case, then you hopefully have an open door policy where you can escalate your concerns higher up the chain.

But be very prudent, because, in my years, I have seen successes in things I initially thought would never work.

14. Those dummies!

When you hear something like, "those guys made a stupid decision," or "they're a bunch of idiots over there," which implies that when given a task, or when faced with a decision or a choice to take actions "those people" were imbeciles and need to be fired. There were times when I was upset and frustrated over some person or people's work or actions or decisions, but I can't recall ANY time, in my entire career and dealing with many people/groups throughout EDS, when after looking further into the matter, that this was caused by stupidity or irresponsibility.

After finding out the full story, and again in my experience, there has always been a reasonable explanation. What might appear to be "stupid" behavior may be caused by rushed or inadequate training, or requirements that were not communicated accurately, etc. Maybe the originally agreed upon action to be taken had to be replaced by an alternative action because of unforeseen circumstances, but there was no time available to adjust adequately, and where "no action" or any "delayed action" would have caused a much more serious problem.

My experience has shown that by far people are dedicated to their job and their team, and work hard and do their best to do a good job. Although the comment "those idiots" can sometimes be common in the workplace, by casting such hasty judgments on people in these situations, you could cause unfair and maybe irreparable harm. It certainly diminishes the overall company's sense of teamwork. Again, you never look in only one direction before crossing the street. So for anyone, but especially as a manager, always be open and fair as to the underlying reasons, when faced with problems or actions that disappoint you.

This also means that you are not at the mercy of stupid/irresponsible behavior or actions, but that you can take steps to minimize these situations – better training, better communication, or simply greater understanding and tolerance when unexpected things happen.

15. You will be incredibly busy and stretched almost all the time.

I remember that I used to joke with my team of leaders, and this was for all the years that I was a manager of a team or a large organization: "Man, I thought I was busy yesterday!" But I also used to say, "Boy, it's always so busy and stressful, but I just love my job!" and that was the absolute truth! I loved the challenges, having to find solutions to difficult and complex organizational and people problems, the project successes, and the satisfaction of recognizing/rewarding/advancing deserving people.

And that's with having to face things that were deathly frightening, like having to prepare and present sometimes good, sometimes not so good, and sometimes terrible news to very large groups of people who reported to me. It also includes having to reprimand people, or denying requests for raises, or having to terminate people's employment. Be prepared for a whirlwind of responsibilities, activities you'll need to be involved with, decisions you'll need to make, and actions you'll need to take.

The good news is that you'll be able to adjust to it, and you will be able to handle it.

16. Get used to being criticized.

The higher you move up in management, the greater the likelihood that you will be open to criticism. This can create disappointment, hurt, and even fear of making mistakes. This is another aspect of management and leadership that you'll have to deal with very personally.

If you perform your work, take actions, and make decisions based primarily upon how you'll be perceived or possibly criticized, you will not be successful as a leader, because you'll then eventually and repeatedly make decisions to avoid criticism, at the expense of what is best for the project, customer, or organization.

The reality is that you'll eventually have to make "tough" or very "unpopular" decisions, or have to carry out unpopular decisions that are made for you by upper management.

The following are some examples of having to give people bad news that open you up to criticism:

- Ask your team to work late to make a project deadline.

- Ask your team to work the weekend, or even worse, to be ready for an upcoming "death march," where there will be weeks or even a month or more of extremely long hours, weekend work, and even all-nighters to meet project or contract commitments. And for those who might be thinking "well, that's simply an example of poor planning or poor project management," let me just say that even if you are the world's best project manager/planner, sh*t does and will happen.

- Need a certain person or persons to go on a month-long temporary duty (TDY) assignment out of state for a high priority project because they have the needed skills, knowing that they have a spouse and children.

- Ask a certain person or persons to go on a multi-month TDY, knowing they recently returned from a grueling TDY assignment.

- Ask people to go on TDY, and they are concerned that you select them because they are single and don't have a family, and this contributes to them being single.

- Inform people: "We will not be able to pay for all the training that we would want. This will leave a great deal of room for self-investment, self-development, and self-direction – don't expect your manager to make you more valuable – your manager will help, but it is primarily up to you."

- Can't give a top employee a perk or bonus for their exceptional work on a successful project because of budget cuts.

- Inform your entire organization that there will be no salary increases this year, possibly longer, with the benefit being that we can hopefully fend off layoffs.

- Inform someone that they can't work from home.

- Inform someone or a number of people who are working from home that they need to start reporting back to the office – no exceptions.

- Inform someone that you have selected someone else for a long desired and deserving opportunity or promotion, and instead selected someone whom you felt was more deserving.

- Inform someone that they are being terminated because they are not performing at the required level.

- Inform someone or people that because of cost reductions, they are part of a pool of people, meaning they are the lowest ranked performers/contributors, who are being terminated.

- Inform a team of people that due to corporate-wide head-count reductions, you are closing their entire office and they are all losing their jobs, and it has nothing to do with poor performance.

Besides the deep impact on the employees and their families with scenarios like the above, remember that most of these will be face-to-face one-on-ones with people, and besides the receiver of this news, it can be deeply painful for you as the manager as well. Actions like these and the potential criticisms can be harsh, so you'll have to be able to cope – and you will with time.

Although these things will burden you, will be constantly on your mind and may cause you to lose sleep, you'll come in to the office the next day or the next week, and be presented with a new set of priority problems and challenges that will require your full and immediate attention, and 100% of your focus.

17. Be prepared to have your opinions and decisions questioned or challenged.

First of all, never think that everyone will agree with you. I've been completely shocked on a number of occasions, on people having contrary opinions on things I thought were absolute "slam dunks." I also used to have an almost instinctive sense that you do not question or challenge the person in charge. It would be a no-no for me to question my manager on a decision – it would be extremely disrespectful. I would feel even worse if someone on my team disagreed with me – it was almost like they were going against me personally. Now I would never strike back in retribution but would be initially hurt by it. Like so many other aspects of management, I had to learn to not take it so personally when people disagreed or challenged my opinions.

When I came to SoCal as a supervisor, I couldn't believe the first time I saw another supervisor, not only disagree but actually fervently argue with our manager. Now they had worked together at another account for many years before, but that was a real eye-opener for me. To be clear, there was no screaming and yelling, but still, I thought, oh my, this guy is going to get fired.

I learned though that it was not seen at all as gross disrespect by that manager, but rather only a healthy disagreement. The manager kind of smiled and then emphatically rebutted with his points. From that experience, my threshold or tolerance for having people disagree with me went up several notches, where strong opinions could be shared very professionally, and thoughtfully considered, without having to escalate into heated arguments.

I also learned that in this California work environment, people were more likely to question you with "whys?" This State was much more of an employee-friendly state from a legal standpoint, meaning there was greater sensitivity to ensuring that employees were treated well and fairly, so people had a greater sense of their rights. This was pretty much the work environment in which I spent most of my career as an organizational and people manager.

They were more likely to question things, push-back, disagree, and criticize decisions, so you had to be prepared to discuss the aspects of your position if needed.

But also, and as importantly, as the manager, you have to remember that you don't need everyone's approval or agreement. You can never forget that you are in charge, and you make the final decisions. Managing "is not a democracy" as we also learned in early EDS leadership training. It's still important and valuable to gather a lot of input, have open discussions, even gain consensus, but in the end, the final decision, the consequences of any decision, and accountability rest on your shoulders.

It's a balancing act. You need to create and maintain a safe environment for your people and your leaders where anyone can openly put forth their ideas, or express their concerns without fear of being criticized or of any retribution. Just remember that at some point, you'll have to make a decision and go with it.

18. Slow to address concerns.

I touched upon this earlier in "Tips for Working With Your Manager" regarding having reasonable expectations on how quickly your manager can get to an issue that you've presented. This provides a little more depth on this matter.

As a manager, you always have to address any valid issues as quickly as possible. The more serious the problem, the greater the speed and focus with which you will need to address the matter.

But be aware that often there may be operational time constraints impacting your availability and ability to address these issues promptly. While you have to deal with pressing concerns that are brought to your attention by your staff, the daily work and operational demands don't remain static.

When addressing one important concern, you may get one or more priority customer or project issues that come up, or the last minute demand from your manager at headquarters for a critical budget analysis that's due on Monday, or you need to roll-out the last minute and large organization change, or even, yup, a new corporate-wide time tracking system. Your people may sometimes complain why it's taking you so long to fix a problem that they brought to your attention, not knowing that you have competing priorities with critical implementation time requirements.

Sometimes the priority that is taking so much of your time has to remain confidential as well so you can't even provide an explanation.

You may simply have to suck it up, do the best you can, accept that some people will be dissatisfied even when you get to it because you took so long.

19. The good and bad of Annual Employee Surveys.

I could devote an entire chapter on this, but in a nutshell, there have been many impactful benefits to the team and organization as a result of acquiring information, input, and recommendations from these surveys, but there's always a flip side to everything. You don't often hear about these aspects, so it's to make you aware and somewhat prepared.

There was a time when all EDS accounts were given a statistical Employee Survey Index (ESI) or score, essentially employee satisfaction scores, which were then rolled up to Regions, Divisions, Strategic Business Units, and Corporate. If your company has these surveys, besides getting scores and input on general operational matters, you'll likely get input about yourself as the manager.

It's great to hear good feedback about yourself from people, very helpful to learn of areas in which you can and need to improve, but emotionally draining at times to receive some very piercing although helpful, and sometimes spiteful feedback. I know some leaders who received comments that were devastating to them – all anonymously. And EDS always made it very clear that any kind of retaliation, especially from a manager, was a fireable offense.

Just remember that if you receive such criticism, whether from a formal employee survey or not, learn from it, you can survive it, and you'll eventually get over it.

Whatever you do, don't quit over it.

20. Keep your people updated and informed on what you're trying to achieve, especially in difficult times.

Here's an example, from a different perspective, on when your staff turns to you for direction, information, and guidance. We were almost always in a multi-story office building, and when the fire alarm went off, everyone evacuated to the parking lot or lawn, and if it was not a scheduled drill, it was always the case that no one knew what was going on.

It always amazed me, and to this day, how people in charge don't seem to have the sense or procedures in place to keep people apprised as to what is happening. There were hundreds of people, from up to 30 floors, and no one from building management would make an effort to inform people. A megaphone would have been extremely helpful. There's confusion; people are asking around for any information on what's going on, wondering how long they have to be out there, when can they go back in because they had to leave from a conference room without their car keys.

What I had done in the past was to set up a procedure where someone from my office (one person, in particular, was always on the ball with things like this) would make her way to wherever the building management folks were and find out what was going on, then get back to me with the information. Then I'd give an update to people from my office on the situation, the reason for the alarm, how long it might take, etc. What I found was that people from other offices would gather around to get the scoop because no one else was keeping them informed.

This is to highlight the value of keeping your people informed through simple communication. It alleviated some of the confusion and uncertainty, provided some timeframe on how long this situation will last, and to move everyone to a safer area if needed.

But this example can also be representative of what is occurring in your office on a daily basis. Do people know what's going on, is it clear what their priorities should be, or might there be any confusion? Maybe there's no confusion but are you sure they are working on the priority aspects of your business? Are they properly motivated and incented to optimize their productivity and efficiency? It is your responsibility to ensure that everyone is provided with the necessary information and direction to move forward in a coordinated, efficient, and orchestrated manner to obtain optimal results. It starts with you understanding the key components of your business and setting achievable goals and measures.

Here are two slides from a presentation that I gave to my account team on June 28, 1999, discussing how we all needed to work in a coordinated manner to ensure all aspects of our business were aligned to achieve our goals. It was a reminder that we can't only focus on the work in front of us. We always have to take time to get out of the weeds and be mindful of the business from the grandstands to make sure we're all working

So You Want To Be A Manager   77

to move in the same direction and in a coordinated manner. This was during a time of significant corporate restructuring and layoffs.

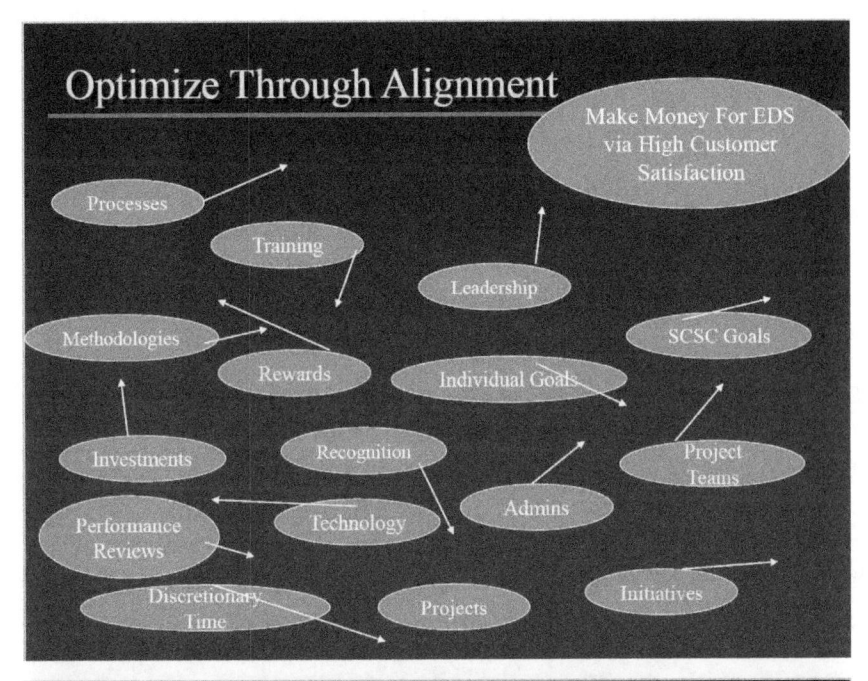

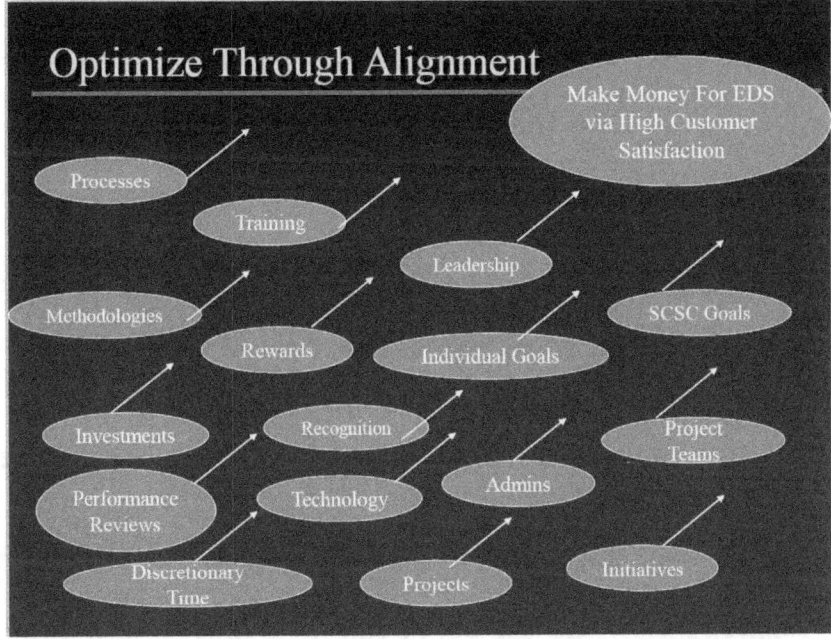

![Optimize Through Alignment diagram — before and after views showing nodes such as Processes, Training, Leadership, Methodologies, Rewards, Individual Goals, SCSC Goals, Investments, Recognition, Project Teams, Performance Reviews, Technology, Admins, Discretionary Time, Projects, and Initiatives, all aligning toward "Make Money For EDS via High Customer Satisfaction"]

21. Establish and communicate your expectations.

It is also important to ensure that everyone on your staff understands your expectations, so you need to write it down, communicate and discuss it, and adjust as you deem necessary. To illustrate, "MY BELIEFS AND EXPECTATIONS" in the section below is something I sent out to all my leaders and discussed in a leadership meeting in 1999.

At the time I had seven managers reporting to me, with a total staff of 115. It's important to note that my leaders were already experienced, people caring, motivated, strong leaders with whom I depended upon every day, and with whom I would trust with my life.

I had shared versions of this with them before, but still felt that it was important to communicate this, so everyone was clearly on the same page regarding my core beliefs and expectations, and my desired direction for them to lead the people in their organizations, and the entire account. This was more on the People side. We had our Business and Financial targets as well.

MY BELIEFS AND EXPECTATIONS
Meeting With My Leaders
Norm Oshiro, updated 11/3/99

BELIEFS:

1. People should be challenged.
2. People should enjoy coming to work.
3. People deserve to be treated with respect.
4. A leader should have a sincere concern for his/her people (career and personal).
5. A leader should always work to create a positive and supportive environment.
6. People thrive in an encouraging environment and this should be fostered and maintained. However, positive feedback only is not in the best interest of the individual.

There should always be feedback on areas for improvement.

7. With support and encouragement, people need to be stretched and developed beyond their expectations – beyond what they ever thought they could do themselves.

8. People must take primary responsibility for their career development and for increasing their value to the account and corporation.

MY EXPECTATIONS OF MY LEADERS:
PROJECT

1. SEI/CMM Level 2 processes – Demonstrate solid skills in planning, organizing, and controlling projects – good contingency planning.

2. Your customers should be very well informed as to our accomplishments, concerns, plans (major milestones met or people put in a long weekend, upcoming vacations, training classes, etc.).

3. Keep me informed of project status, concerns, progress, etc.

4. Be the first to inform me of problems and successes.

PROCEDURAL

1. Demonstrate good follow-through on all assignments, questions, requests - keep me posted regularly on progress and/or delays.

2. Ensure that performance appraisals are well researched (more emphasis on customer, peer, and project leader feedback than on "checklist" type of things the individual did), and administered on time.

3. Salary schedule guidelines are monitored (you make the judgment call on requesting more/less, sooner/later), write-ups are well researched (answers "so what?") and submitted on time.

4. Be prompt at meetings.

5. Demonstrate healthy discontent.

6. Question the status quo.

7. Don't hesitate to openly disagree with me or anyone else on the Leadership Team.
8. After consensus is reached and/or a decision is made, need to get fully behind it.
9. Demonstrate a positive, cooperative, and supportive attitude.
10. Manage vacations, carry-over.
    - Plan to minimize the impact on the project.
    - The customer kept informed.
    - Minimize carry-over vacation.

PEOPLE

1. Consistently promote a positive/supportive work environment.
2. Each person knows the direction and status of the project, and their purpose and responsibilities at all times.
3. Have your Leader candidates and those aspiring to be leaders, promote account team building and company pride building. They should set an example for others. It is not enough to only lead/manage projects if they want to progress in the Leadership career path.
4. People are periodically reminded that they are important and valued by you and the project.
5. You challenge your people and make them take primary responsibility for their career development and increasing their value to this account/EDS.
6. Assist your people in their career development.
7. Appropriate people are informed and coached when performance drops. Update me as appropriate.
8. You constantly look for reasons to pat your people on the back – please keep me abreast also.
9. Be proactive in getting perks for your deserving people.
10. Be proactive in acquiring customer perks/bonuses for your people when appropriate.

11. Introduce new people to everyone at the account.

GENERAL

1. Identify and leverage pockets of untapped value.
2. Make decisions based on value creation.
3. Demonstrate a high level of self-motivation.
4. Care about your people.
5. Be able to work well with others.
6. Demonstrate professionalism in conduct and appearance at all times.
7. Demonstrate strong delegation skills.
8. Show initiative and creativity ("what if we did this, or try this?").
9. Have a sense of humor.
10. Able to overcome hurdles and solve problems.
11. Able to utilize a variety of PC tools.
12. Able to develop a strong cohesive team.
13. Able to build support for EDS, the account, and the Leadership team.

QUESTIONS FOR YOU:

1. What are your expectations of me?
2. What do you enjoy about what you're doing?
3. What don't you like?
4. Is there anything you are concerned or worried about?
5. What else would you like to be doing that you're not doing now?
6. What motivates you?
7. What are your career goals?
8. What classes would you like to take?

Responsibility and Accountability

It's important to note that the material I present in this book does not represent the results of my coming into a poorly run and unprofessional organization, and by cracking the whip with all my knowledge and experience on leadership, was able to transform this organization into a highly productive and professional organization. That was definitely not the case. I was fortunate to have come into an already highly professional, and highly productive organization that had been shaped and run by very sharp, very caring, and highly ethical leaders.

Most of what is in this book come from what I learned and experienced on the job over the 32 plus years with EDS, from working with excellent people and excellent managers, and from EDS' leadership training.

1. A lesson I learned as a kid.

I once saw an adult not own up to something he did. It was a small matter but even at about seven years old, it made a lasting impression on me. It was at the service station which a relative owned, where one of my uncles was working on an engine. He stepped away, and one of the guys who was there observing, moved a certain part closer thinking it would help. When my uncle came back, and the part wasn't where he left it, he asked: "hey, I just left this right here, who moved it?" The guy who moved it was close by and heard, but didn't say anything. Again, it seems like a small thing, but I lost a lot of respect for that person, from that day on.

He didn't have the honesty to admit to what he had done.

2. A good lesson I learned as a kid.

One day an older cousin of mine, who was one of my role models, took me dove hunting in Kawaihae, on the sunny side of the Big Island so that I could get some bird hunting experience – he had also taken me wild pig hunting way up mauka in the Panaewa Rainforest. On this dove trip, a bird flew by so he tracked it and fired. He missed, but the pellet spray arched down and apparently fell on another hunter who was farther away but out of view. He didn't get hurt, but got pissed-off, stood up and yelled out "eh, who shot that?!" We now could see him, but he couldn't see us, and my cousin could have simply not said anything, but he stood up, waved to the guy saying "over here" until he saw us, then said "sorry!"

The guy gruffly said OK and sat back down, and we couldn't see him again, but that was a huge lesson to me on owning up and taking responsibility, even if you couldn't be seen and could have gotten away with it.

3. As a manager, you need to hold yourself accountable for your actions, behaviors, and performance.

This means that when you screw up, even if it's a little thing, take responsibility. Tell those who were negatively impacted that you're sorry and feel bad about it. This could be a teammate, your team, your boss, or your customer.

Give thought to how you will rectify the situation and prevent it from happening again so you can communicate this at the same time. But the main first step is the sincere apology. Depending on the severity, you might say, "I'm really sorry about that," or "hey folks, I'm really sorry about that" – show, first and foremost, that you are owning up to your mistake, and that you sincerely feel bad about it. Then if actions need to be taken, communicate what you are going to do about it.

If your mistake was a huge one, then everything needs to get ratcheted up.

4. Holding your people accountable.

Holding yourself accountable is essential, but one of the most important and toughest parts of your job will be to hold your people accountable if they don't meet your expectations, or for demonstrating undesirable actions or behaviors. You are responsible for affecting people's actions and behaviors, so they are in line with company standards and your expectations. It's very important to remember that your success in holding people accountable and changing undesirable behaviors, is dependent upon whether you deliver immediate and certain consequences, or delayed and uncertain consequence, or no consequences at all.

Don't put off having a needed discussion with your employee, or wait for a six month or annual performance review. Again, you will get what you tolerate.

Sometimes, it may be obvious that the person knows they missed the mark and clearly feels bad about it – nothing may need to be said. But other times, you'll need to point this out to the person.

There are two parts to this. The first is the individual needs to clearly understand that you have expectations and will hold them accountable for not meeting performance standards or for their undesirable action.

The second is the resulting impact on the team when they see that you have the mettle to take up the issue directly with the individual. It can be demoralizing for team members if they see that people can get away with bad or unprofessional behavior or poor performance. This is not to say that you call people out in public, or berate them, but if you are consistent with having a one-on-one to discuss these issues, word will get around that everyone is being held to the same standard.

And this is not to instill fear – in the workplace, there should be more pats-on-the-back for good work than reprimands – but when you consistently hold people accountable, respect for meeting expectations will become the culture.

Again, for some, confronting people in situations like this may not be difficult. But for most who are moving up in leadership, it's not easy. You might even be scared sh*tless, which will make it very easy for you to avoid what you need to do, by giving yourself excuses, or rationalizing why you don't need to do it.

I believe that many people falter or fail in leadership because they choose the avoidance path in these situations. The only way to overcome this challenge is to push through and just do it. Being nervous, or terrified with cold and shaking hands, and a shaky voice even, is secondary. If you have to, write down what needs to be corrected and why, so you don't blank out, but deliver your message to the person one-on-one, or on the phone one-on-one if they are remote.

You're the manager, you are clear on your expectations, so it's not a debate, and it's not a negotiation. Again, if you are worried that you'll come across as nervous, scared, or weak, even if that's the case, that is secondary – do it! I assure you, you will gain more respect among your employees, you will respect yourself more, and it will get easier over time.

Balance these difficult situations with understanding, fairness, and recognition of your people at other times.

5. Attempts don't count.

You'll often be responsible for getting something done but will have to depend on others for component pieces. You are not relieved of responsibility if you are waiting for needed pieces and have calls out to the individual who owes you something.

Having three calls out with voicemail messages attempting to get the deliverables with no word back doesn't cut it. Your responsibility is to get the job done so don't tell your boss "he never called me back" or "there was no way to get in touch with him." If you've exhausted all the options you had available, ask someone for help, call the person's team leader or manager, or proactively take it to your manager so he/she can take action by escalating this to the person's management.

Your job is done only when the job is complete.

6. Accountability on matrixed teams.

Special management challenges are presented when people from different managers, and who therefore don't report to you organizationally, are assigned to your project team, particularly when some or all of them are geographically dispersed. See "Accountability on matrixed project teams" under "Project Management" for a detailed discussion.

7. A non-confrontational method to hold a person's feet to the fire.

On one project where the team was remotely dispersed, I had an experienced person who I hadn't worked with before, who seemed a little lax on getting his tasks done. These situations did not happen very often, but it can happen more often with remote teams where you can't simply pop in to see the person day in and day out.

This was a priority project, so I had established daily morning meetings via conference call, to ensure everything was on track. To resolve this issue, I simply made sure to ask each person for the status of their key deliverables in these meetings. Everyone was on top of their work and provided crisp updates, except this one individual.

After the 2nd day of my asking, with this person again reporting slow progress, he got the message that I was going to be asking him the same question the next day, and the next. He sharpened up, and never got behind again. Peer-pressure added some needed motivation, without the need for me to have a one-on-one with him, or for me to have to contact his manager to discuss the issue. It became uncomfortable and unacceptable to himself, to be the only one not getting his work done on time.

8. **Accountability escalation:**

- Make sure your expectations are well defined and understood.

- If someone falls short of expectations but clearly knows it and is remorseful, you may not need to say anything.

- If it happens again, you need to immediately bring it to the person's attention.

- If an action, behavior, or performance significantly misses the mark, you need to address this with the individual immediately.

- If you don't take action, this or something similar will very likely happen again, and even worse from a team perspective, others will see that you will let these things slide because you don't have the nerve to address it directly with the person, which will be a de-motivator for the team, especially for your top performers.

- Confirm with the individual that they will indeed deliver what you asked, with a specific date and time.

- Ask for periodic updates, so there's no non-delivery surprise.
- If you don't get the deliverable when promised, it may be time to initiate a formal work improvement plan. This is basically listing the needed deliverable(s) with delivery date(s), which also specifies the consequence (potential separation from employment) for not meeting the deliverables, with signature lines for the manager, employee, and possibly a witness. It does not matter if the employee chooses not to sign it. In my experience, initiating such a plan was extremely rare.
- If the problem persists, this person may not be a match for your organization.
- If the individual fails to meet the requirements of the work improvement plan, it will be grounds for termination.

Again, holding people accountable, meaning you are having to confront people personally to address unacceptable behavior or poor performance, will be a critical part of your job as a manager.

By setting clear expectations and consistently holding people to them, over time, you should get to the point where you will be able to trust all the people you depend upon, things run more efficiently, and this will allow you and your team to be better able to deal with critical business, project, and organizational challenges. This can help you take an already highly professional and productive organization and achieve even greater things. At that point, having to "hold people accountable" should represent a minimal part of your job.

When I left the SE Center to move into the Sales group, our center had been assessed per the Carnegie Mellon's Systems Engineering Institute, Capability Maturity Model (SEI/CMM) as a Level 2 organizational. This was a globally recognized achievement at the time.

We were also among the first five SE Centers in the company to adopt and be operational in the corporate mandated Global Solution Center Model (GSCM) which was SEI/CMM compliant, we had people training other centers worldwide in a critical GSCM component, and we were approaching readiness to be assessed at SEI/CMM Level 3 maturity. At that time there were

62 EDS SE or solution centers worldwide, we were one of 24 which had been assessed at Level 2, one of five centers which were operating under GSCM, and there was only one center that had reached Level 3 which was an SE Center in India.

I was fortunate to have experienced this, it was at the highest point of my organizational management career with EDS, which extended into most of the year 2000, and it reflected the caliber and quality of my leadership team, administrative assistants, and the entire SoCal SE Center staff. And we were just one small representative sample of the hundreds of teams and organizations throughout EDS.

CHAPTER 4: MANAGEMENT RESPONSIBILITIES

Context

This chapter covers what I've found to be some of the most critical responsibilities and challenges that you'll face once you become a Manager, and as I've done previously in the book, I offer suggested "how to's" to deal with some of them.

There are a wide range and many different elements to management, but I touch upon just a few of them.

As examples, these are some of the performance evaluation components for managers, against which we were measured over the years: managing financials (budgeting, profit & loss), achieving goals, team building, support of upper management, industry knowledge, delegating, delivering services, customer commitment, problem solving, managing complexity, motivational, inspiring, visionary, communication skills, creativity, quality, integrity, negotiating, performance under pressure, business sense, planning, innovative, risk-taking, decision-making, protecting company assets, marketing, and also employee turn-over rate.

These were not measures for managers in a single performance review, but criteria from different times and from different groups over the years, to give you some perspective on the scope of management.

Although management responsibilities are wide-ranging, and I touch upon only a small portion in this book, you can better wrap your mind around its expanse by looking at the commonly referenced Five Management Functions. These were also covered in one of my EDS leadership classes many years ago.

The Five Management Functions:
1. Planning
2. Organizing
3. Staffing
4. Directing/Leading
5. Controlling

This should provide some structure for your continued study in the area of Management, so research these topics further on your own.

Again, I touch upon only a small slice of "Management" in this book, but I cover aspects that stood out to me as being critical, and among the most difficult to fulfill in my role as a manager. The topics I cover come from many years of experience working with people and teams, and the challenges that we faced every day.

Business Ethics

Code of Conduct

EDS had a strict written business code of conduct called "EDS Corporate Ethics: A Code of Conduct, Your Responsibility".

Before being formally hired, we were required to read it. From the very start with EDS, we were taught Business Ethics, honesty, and fairness. Ross Perot espoused and demanded that all EDS employees were to always operate within the "bull's-eye" of ethical behavior – never outside nor on the fringes of the bull's-eye – and not ever to have even the appearance of being on the fringes. This was ingrained in us, and I remember sitting through training classes and videos where they highlighted real-life examples of unethical and even unlawful behavior by a few employees.

This is why I admired Ross, loved the company, and the reason, as I mentioned earlier, why I was willing to sell our house and move my family, from our home in Hawaii to the mainland so that I could build a career with EDS. I was always proud to be a part of this company, through all its ups and downs, and it was primarily because of the people with whom I worked.

If you haven't already, you need to learn and understand your company's Code of Conduct, or Code of Business Conduct, or Code of Ethics, and make sure you follow it. Always be ethical in your behavior. You don't want to be on the evening news being asked why you were caught in some business scandal. The point, of course, is not to avoid being caught but to always strive to be an ethical and fair manager for the benefit of your employees and your company. Employees should and deserve to be proud of their company, and that becomes difficult to do if the leaders of the company don't operate and behave ethically.

Also see EDS' Open Door Policy later in this book. It was always impressed upon us to make employees aware of this policy, to encourage its use, and that the consequence would be severe if any leader impeded its use. To be clear, we understood that if a manager prevented an employee from using the Open Door Policy in any way or inflicted retribution on anyone using the Open Door Policy, they would be fired on the spot.

Hiring and Firing

1. Make sure to do your due diligence when hiring people.

Don't be hasty and take shortcuts. Fully research your candidates, follow up on references, do the background checks and drug testing, or use a reputable and trusted third-party firm to do this. Have key people on your team participate in the interview or interviews as the person's skill set and team chemistry are critical components. Do your homework on best-in-class interviewing techniques, use open-ended questions, ask "what would you do in this situation?" etc. Test them in the technical job skills for which you are hiring. Red flags are generally show-stoppers, but also be careful with yellow flags, things that may cause a little hesitancy in the assessments and interviews by you or your team – things you might think will be easy to work through, or things you think shouldn't be a problem or a big deal.

Little things can translate into very big problems after the person is hired.

2. Keep in mind that hiring mistakes are almost always a major hassle, including potential legal liability.

Correcting hiring mistakes will be time-consuming, more than you can probably imagine. It can be such a negative impact on the team; it can cause/create a lot of stress in the workplace; it can create a lot of legal headaches for you, and can be a productivity and psychological drain.

Being with EDS, a large corporation, we had a safety net with EDS Employee Relations and EDS Legal support. If we ever had any employee related issues, we could call in to corporate and first get expert advice from legal assistants. If there was any risk of legal action against us, we could work with attorneys from EDS Legal. These resources were a huge help especially being in California as this was/is a strong employee-rights state. They didn't only help us with problems, they provided information and guidance to avoid trouble (how to handle unused vacation days, vacation carry-over, over-time, time recording, tax liability for perks and bonuses, tax implications if people were TDY on

Management Responsibilities

projects out of state for months at a time, independent contractor (1099) vs. employee issues, etc.

> *I had a situation one year when we brought someone onboard as an independent contractor for a certain skill set and for a specific project. She did good work, but after the project ended and she was fully paid, she took us to court, claiming she was an employee and demanded back-benefits to be paid to her. It took hours upon hours to prepare for the case, gathering up our documentation, including her project assignments, deliverables, timesheets, and the initially signed agreement. We also spent hours working with EDS Legal to prepare. The judge, after hearing both sides and reviewing the former contractor's documentation and then our documentation, quickly ruled in our favor. Upon leaving the proceedings, we ended up in the same crowded elevator and next to each other where the person smiled at me, shrugged her shoulders, and said: "well, you gotta try right?"*

So even though you have strict procedures and tightly worded agreements even prepared by corporate legal, you can still get mired in time and resource draining work to defend yourself if anyone decides to challenge you, and this gets piled on top of all the other work you already have on your plate. As a manager, you and your administrative staff need to keep good records and documentation.

3. Employee terminations.

Make sure you have documented evidence supporting your decision to terminate someone's employment. A good way to approach this is to assume that you will have to go to court and your "evidence" will be presented to and reviewed by a judge. The judge will also be getting counter-arguments from the other side, and will then make a final determination. You do not want to submit sloppy, hastily put together, or incomplete documentation. That means documentation should have started back at the time of your initial concerns – describing what happened and with dates and times. Tap your managers and use whatever company resources you may have at your disposal to ensure you have your ducks in a row.

At the time of the separation, follow your company's separation procedures, have a witness or security present if necessary, keep the meeting extremely brief, avoid any unnecessary discussions, collect company items like the security access badge, and you should have planned out the exact physical movements of the individual from that room or office to the point they are out of the building. Building security should have already been alerted.

After the person has left, document everything that happened. It doesn't necessarily have to be so cold, but your starting point should be very conservative, precise, and professional.

I've done separations that were somewhat friendly with a warm handshake, a goodbye and "take good care," to escorting the person from my office, through the building, and out the exit without a word said. I never felt the need for security, in any of the separations I performed, but that was a long time ago now.

I've had to separate a few people for poor performance. On the one hand, there was an employee that was not pulling his weight on the team, which required others to pick up the slack. I conducted one-on-ones with this person alerting him of my concerns, which escalated to a formal warning, then to a work improvement plan, but it was obvious to everyone that this individual was not putting out an aggressive effort to get his work done and I finally had to separate him from the company.

In another situation, I had to terminate someone from my project team who would do anything he could to help anyone with anything. He was inherently friendly and had the greatest attitude, was always the first at work, put in among the longest hours, and was always among the last to leave. You could clearly see that he was always trying his hardest and putting in a lot of time and effort to support the project. However, technically, he was not doing satisfactory work, kept falling behind, and became a burden to his teammates who had to pick up some of his assignments. "Effort" does not always translate into "results," and getting results is what matters. Having to sit down with him to let him go was one of the hardest things I had to do. I remember getting choked up about this in front of the entire team when I made the announcement that I had to let him go. The separation was clearly justified, but still very difficult to do, and I'm not forgetting the huge negative impact on the people I terminated and their families. See the Chapter "My Worst Experiences as a Manager" for my worst separation experience.

Rewards and Recognition

1. Be consistent in rewarding and recognizing people.

It is your responsibility to recognize and reward your people for good work, positive results, and for exhibiting the type of good behaviors you want from your people. This could include sharing their technical expertise to support their teammates, staying late to help out a co-worker who is coming up to speed, volunteering to find a solution to some pressing technical issue, or keeping people's spirits up during a grueling project, etc.

There should be ample opportunities for you to pop into someone's cube to let them know that you appreciated what they've done, or to call them into your office to do the same, or to send them a simple email acknowledgment. But when you single people out for recognition in a more public setting, you always need to view this from a broader perspective – what impact is it having among the other employees. Are you being fair, are you forgetting someone, and what expectations are you setting for the future?

When you praise people, give thought to other employees to see if you maybe missed recent opportunities. It may be hard to go back, but this will help you avoid a similar missed opportunity in the future. Also, recognition needs to be earned. If your threshold is too low, it becomes too easy, and it loses its value. There's a balancing act involved in almost all aspects of management.

With experience, it gets easier to strike that balance.

When giving out more substantive awards, or perks, or bonuses, you need to make doubly sure that you are fair and consistent, because you will be setting bigger expectations for everyone else.

You should always have dollars budgeted to reward your people. If you are new in your leadership job, find out from your management what options and constraints you have on recognition – thousands of dollars, a few hundred dollars, less than a hundred, or zero dollars.

I've had all of these limitations over the years. So recognition could range from bonus/cash awards, perks like tickets to the movies or the Supercross, a dinner out, a couple of paid days off, a training class, sincere personal thank yous with a letter/email, acknowledgement in a team or company meeting, an open letter of thanks to your employee sent to your manager to give visibility to your employee with upper management, and even the rare stock options. Do your homework on any tax implications and make the employee aware up front. You don't want to give your employee a gift certificate for $400, and they then find their next paycheck surprisingly light because of taxes withheld.

But above all, be consistent, not just with the people on your team, but across teams and different managers! If one manager gave an employee a $500 perk and you gave a $450 perk for the same or similar contributions, it will cause problems. With bonuses of thousands of dollars, in particular, we always met as a leadership team to review people's contributions in rank order and allocated bonus dollars accordingly.

In my time managing a large organization which was from the early 1990s into the year 2000, amounts were supposed to be held confidential by the employees.

2. Perks.

With perks, we were taught that you need to first do research on the employee's interests, or needs, or favorite places, etc., so you can provide a perk that would be targeted and meaningful and useful to the employee. If you know the individual well and know for certain what they would want or need, then that's great, and you can leverage that knowledge for something special. But if not, in my experience, award the person with something generic or preferably cash/check/bonus, and skip the time-consuming researching that could ultimately result in a disappointment, no matter how much you researched.

A case in point. One employee receiving a perk was an avid fisherman. His manager put in a lot of effort researching every source possible to find the best rod & reel set available, within budget of course, for the employee.

But unless you found out a preference directly from the person, that's like getting an expert photographer the best camera you could find for $1,000. No matter how much research you put into it, you would probably be better off awarding the person a $1,000 perk or bonus so they could find something on their own. Their ultimate purchase might turn out to be totally unrelated to photography, but something really needed at the time, and even more warmly appreciated.

3. Recognizing or introducing people.

When you are presenting a special recognition or even introducing new people, or a special visitor, certainly highlight the achievement if that is the purpose of the meeting, but also use it as an opportunity to brag about them. Promote some of the things that they've done or achieved, or which made them proud, but would never bring up themselves.

I had a Division Manager who was a US Marine Corps Captain in the Vietnam War and who was wounded in combat. I learned this just from a casual conversation at a happy hour event sometime before where he had shared some details. Knowing that it wasn't something that he kept private, I briefly mentioned this as part of my introduction of him when he visited for our account review. I knew it was something meaningful and prideful for him.

> *A quick side story about this division manager. Around that time during one of our trips for a meeting in Texas, he invited his wife to join us for dinner. We were chatting after ordering our meals, and our manager commented about something, where his wife then offered a slightly different perspective on it. He turned to her, raised his voice a little and said: "don't you **ever** contradict me in front of my staff again!" She looked at him, smiled, then rolled her eyes, and after we all were a bit shocked, we then had a very good laugh. It set a fun and pleasant atmosphere for the rest of the evening.*

He was another manager I was lucky to have had for a number of years. He was the one who had given final approval for me to become the SoCal SE Center Manager a few years before.

Once, in a classroom situation where we needed to spend a few minutes getting to know someone at our table, then introduce them, I learned that my female fellow student was a

Harley Davidson owner/rider. I remember talking briefly about what EDS department she was with, her career track so far, and why she was taking the class, but I also talked about her Harley and how much she loved her weekend rides, and I noticed that she was beaming, shyly, but beaming with pride. When introducing her, I talked about her work and career, and all that stuff, but what she most appreciated was my highlighting of her weekend rides on her Harley.

When you recognize or even introduce someone, try to honor them in a way that would make even their family proud. Never stretch the truth but go ahead and brag on their behalf. If you ever have to introduce or honor someone, in writing, or at an event, if possible, get input from the person, or people that know them well, on what he or she might like you to mention.

It will give you an opportunity to highlight some of their proudest moments or most meaningful achievements that you might never have discovered on your own – as long as the recognition is not supposed to be a surprise.

Remember, it's very important to recognize all of your people, whenever it's merited, and you should always be seeking this out. But make a special effort to recognize your top contributors – many are making a special effort to contribute more at work. You always need to give thought to this aspect of management, so your people feel valued and appreciated by you personally. This will help them to connect with you and the company, and will also help you to retain your people.

By you leading by example with earned acknowledgments, it also creates a culture which is self-sustaining and self-enhancing. Remember that you may not notice or be aware of your deserving people if you only sit in your cube or office all day, so you have to make a point to seek them out.

You can start by asking your team leaders, project managers, and some of your known top performers on who they observe to be stepping up.

The benefit to you? Besides maintaining and enhancing your people's contributions and good performance, the appreciation and gratitude that you'll sometimes receive from your people will stay with you for the rest of your life.

Rankings and Compensation

1. Employee rankings.

It is important to rank or rate your employees, according to the value that they bring to your business or organization. This may not be as important if you have a small company or team where you may work in the same office or facility every day, but you should still have some level of work performance and expectations of your employees, with some assessment on how your people are measuring up to these expectations.

As the number of employees increases, for example from 10 to 20, or 20 to 40, and greater, rankings become more important to fairly and equitably reward your people for their contributions. As discussed earlier, rewards may be as simple but meaningful as thank-yous and pats-on-the-back, to salary increases and bonuses, to new opportunities and promotions.

If you are not doing this fairly and systematically, then you could be missing opportunities to recognize your deserving employees, or demotivating your top performers, and possibly openly tolerating poor performance. If you are not in some way ranking your people, you may not be consistently rewarding them fairly. Furthermore, you will not, in the long run, be getting the very best from your employees, you could be perpetuating low or mediocre performance, and you may eventually lose your best people.

2. Layoffs.

If you are ever forced to reduce your staff, as we were mandated by corporate starting in the mid-1990s, whether it is called workforce reductions, reductions in force, job cuts, down-sizing, right-sizing, or realignments, and you actually have to decide on who you are going to let go, rankings become critical. You don't want to "take your best shot at it" when laying people off, or wing it, then have serious regrets after rethinking it, and after it's too late.

Knowing that you had established ranking criteria to assess people's value to be as fair as possible, does help to put your mind a bit at ease as the decision maker in an already difficult

Management Responsibilities

situation. This also helps to ensure that you are retaining your best people so you can ultimately improve your organization's performance going forward. In the near-term, there will be significant challenges due to the terrible impact of teammates that lost their jobs that hangs over you, the psychological impact on the remaining people, and the fact that they will have to pick up the extra workload.

Situations like these were among the toughest part of the job as a manager.

This is how it was in my experience with EDS, especially in the mid-1990s to 2000 when I was an organizational manager having to initiate layoffs throughout my organization and to conduct layoffs myself. People always had to up their game to bring value, or they could be on the next round of layoffs. I faced a layoff myself two years after I left that SE center management role while in the sales group, and layoffs continued throughout the rest of my career with EDS/HP. There wasn't room for poor performance or complacency in the workplace.

Now I never worked hard to avoid being laid off, maybe I was overly optimistic thinking that I could always land on my feet, but layoffs were a constant reality, and rankings were most often used.

3. Ranking people.

To rank your people, you must have either first-hand knowledge of their work, performance, and contributions, and/or, gather input from those who have. Do not depend only on your own observations, but additionally, acquire input from teammates, team leaders, project managers, and customers, who worked with the individuals.

I have been surprised more than once, especially with a larger organization, to find that an employee whom I thought was doing great work, turned out to have input on the contrary from people who worked closely with this individual. Now it may have still been good work, but not the "stand out" work that I had thought.

This might be short-term results related to a specific task, or due to the technical subject matter, or how the person interacted with teammates or the customer on a particular project – but it involved aspects that you could not have observed first-hand. As surprisingly, individuals who may not have stood out as top performers, did so upon acquiring input.

Also, keep in mind that you have to consider a person's performance and contributions over some length of time. You can't move a person up or down several positions in rankings strictly because of his or her performance on the last assignment or project. It should be based upon sustained performance, from months to even a year or more.

One example might be someone doing really well on a relatively "easy" project, as opposed to someone else, who is usually ranked higher, doing just "OK," but on a very complex project involving a steep learning curve and a new technology. You need to take the time to take these types of variables into consideration. Otherwise, taken on face value, the first person might move up a few spots in the next rankings, and the other might move down, which may not necessarily represent their sustained level of performance and contributions.

4. Ranking criteria.

Using a simple example, if your business produces a single product or component that is put together by your employees, then their performance can be measured by simply tracking how many products they complete, that meet your quality standards, in their shift.

The person who completes the most is at the top of your rankings, and the person with the least is at the bottom. You also want to ensure sustained performance so you would track this monthly, quarterly, annually, etc.

In most jobs, however, it's not that easy. You can't simply count, pick up, and inspect the item produced by each employee. Additionally, each product varies in its complexity and difficulty to produce, and the time it takes to complete. Then there are employees who have a few valuable skills, and others who have a variety of valuable skills. There are still others who not only do their work well, but can pull up the productivity of others by helping them. Others are good at providing training, who can mentor, and also motivate others by encouraging teamwork. Then still others who can better plan, can envision potential problems and have contingencies, who are good at coordinating resources, who can better match tasks with people's skills, and who always improve productivity and work throughput for the entire team.

Then for good measure, throw in interpersonal skills: those who have excellent team and customer skills, those you absolutely keep away from interacting with the customer, and everyone else in between. Then further, you may have employees with a number of different job codes or functions.

So rankings can be complex, but you can start off in a fairly straightforward manner. If you don't have a rankings process with your company, start with your employee performance review criteria. Or create your own, using your best judgment on how you would rate the contributions and value of your employees. Once you get started and rank your people a few times, you'll quickly see how you could adjust it by adding additional criteria or swapping some out.

As an example, the first time you do your rankings, people who you know are your best performers, may not be at the top. This might be a clue that you are missing an important ranking criterion which when added, moves that person up, and would probably affect others.

On the other hand, your rankings may reveal that you have actually been undervaluing some of your people. This is another important reason to do rankings.

To keep things simple at first, let's say you rank each of your employees based on the following three criteria, and the values you assign range from 1 which is the lowest performing value, to 3 which is the highest performing value.

- Productivity
- Technical Skills
- Teamwork

If you want, for values below a 3, you could even go to half point increments so 1.5 or 2.5. You'll be surprised how many times, for an individual, you simply can't rate them at a 2, and a 3 is just a little too high, so a 2.5 is perfect or acceptable.

Your ranking spreadsheet might look like this after inputting the scores for each employee in your first cut, with the scores totaled on the far right "Rank Total":

Ranking Values Entered for Each Employee on a scale from 1 to 3:

Employee	Productivity	Technical Skills	Teamwork	Rank Total
Empl_1	2	2	2	6.0
Empl_2	2.5	2	3	7.5
Empl_3	3	3	2.5	8.5
Empl_4	2.5	2.5	1	6.0
Empl_5	2	2	3	7.0
Empl_6	2	2	1	5.0
Empl_7	3	3	2	8.0
Empl_8	2.5	2.5	3	8.0
Empl_9	2.5	3	2	7.5

After doing a sort on the Rank Total column, your spreadsheet would look like the table below, showing the highest score at the top, Empl_3 who would be ranked #1, and the lowest score on the bottom, Empl_6 who would be ranked #9:

Sorted by Rank Order:

Employee	Productivity	Technical Skills	Teamwork	Rank Total	Ranking
Empl_3	3	3	2.5	8.5	1
Empl_7	3	3	2	8.0	2
Empl_8	2.5	2.5	3	8.0	3
Empl_2	2.5	2	3	7.5	4
Empl_9	2.5	3	2	7.5	5
Empl_5	2	2	3	7.0	6
Empl_1	2	2	2	6.0	7
Empl_4	2.5	2.5	1	6.0	8
Empl_6	2	2	1	5.0	9

It may be what you anticipated, or it may have a few surprises. But it's a starting point to being more quantitative in assessing your employees' value, and more importantly, ensuring that they are being recognized, rewarded, and compensated more equitably, and based on merit.

If you are in a small shop, it can be fairly straightforward as I mentioned earlier. As your organization gets larger, however, with multiple teams, and multiple managers, with additional criteria to encompass the scope of work that your business performs, then add a number of different job functions, and the complexity and time required to do these rankings go up exponentially. When many leaders are involved in the rankings of many employees, everyone needs a shared understanding of each criterion.

However, not everyone will agree on the numerical values given to people. So it's not like you get everyone's separately constructed rankings, consolidate, sort, and you're done. If you want to complete your rankings fast, you could do just that. But in the consolidated version, managers who tend to give higher values could have all of their people up towards the top, and managers who are more conservative could have their people near the bottom.

So to ensure fairness, you should meet to review and discuss. In these rankings meetings leaders will present the rank order of people in their groups. In our final rankings, for example, we ranked all job codes together since they were all within the systems engineering area, where your more senior people should be near the top. There will then be a consolidation of all the groups, discussions of people's contributions, presentation of supporting information, arguments on who is more valuable than someone else, and ultimately gain consensus among the leadership team on the final rank order.

Keep in mind that each leader (say a manager or supervisor) may be "fighting" to place their person or persons above people who are in another leader's team. Here's an option that could save a great deal of time. As opposed to ranking people one above the other from first to last, rank people into "thirds" of the organization, or in "quartiles" – people in the 1st quartile or top 25% in one grouping, in the second 25% in the next grouping, etc. There still are difficulties at the quartile borderlines, but it's much easier to reach an overall consensus than arguing to place people one above the other for everyone on your staff. The whole rankings process is extremely time-consuming because the leaders have to do a lot of homework on their people, and they are doing their best to represent and stand up for their people.

After a few rounds of this though, all the leaders start to pick up on the routine, and the process gets much smoother and faster.

Here are additional examples of ranking criteria we used, to help you create your own. With the list below, you would score your employees in each of the 12 sub-bullets, compared to the 3 that I used in the sample above.

Again, we were in the IT industry, but these are still fairly generic:

Technical Personnel:
- **Job Specific Skills:**
    - Technical
    - Industry Methods & Standards
    - Scope of Influence
    - Process Driven
- **Interpersonal Skills:**
    - Communications
    - Teamwork
- **Customer Focus & Impact:**
    - Customer Focus
    - Customer Satisfaction
- **Leadership Skills:**
    - Leadership
    - Project Management
- **Account Impact:**
    - Account Contributions
    - Track Record of Being Billed to Projects

5. Integrating Rankings with Compensation Management.

Ranking of employees was mandated by corporate in about the mid-1990s. Since I had already started a compensation management spreadsheet for all our employees a few years before, it seemed a logical next step to integrate the rankings numbers into this spreadsheet. Prior to this, we had analyzed individuals and their salaries relative to the top and bottom of their job code salary ranges. These were provided by corporate following industry salary studies. If our best performers were low in the range, we did our best to move them closer to the top of the range.

To see everyone plotted in rank order, against their annual salaries was quite revealing, as organization-wide inequities became immediately clear for the first time. See the sample table and chart below. I started this type of analysis in 1994 and portions of this spreadsheet tool were adopted by EDS' corporate compensation years later.

Some of our top performers were paid below lower ranked people, and some of our highest paid people were not ranked at the top. It also emphasized the discrepancies of people who transferred in from EDS accounts across the country where their cost of living was significantly lower than our Los Angeles area, and where their salary ranges were lower to start with. We, of course, wanted to quickly correct these inequities, but because of corporate limits on percent increases and months between increases, and our committed budgets around salaries and bonuses, it took many months to a few years to get people closer in line with where they should be.

We had to be as aggressive as possible to increase the total compensation (salary, perks, bonuses) for some, and slow down compensation growth for others.

These are examples of what the table and graph would look like after combining Salary with Rankings:

Employee	Productivity	Technical Skills	Teamwork	Rank Total	Salary
Empl_3	3	3	2.5	8.5	$9,000
Empl_7	3	3	2	8.0	$6,000
Empl_8	2.5	2.5	3	8.0	$10,000
Empl_2	2.5	2	3	7.5	$7,500
Empl_9	2.5	3	2	7.5	$7,000
Empl_5	2	2	3	7.0	$3,000
Empl_1	2	2	2	6.0	$4,500
Empl_4	2.5	2.5	1	6.0	$4,000
Empl_6	2	2	1	5.0	$5,000

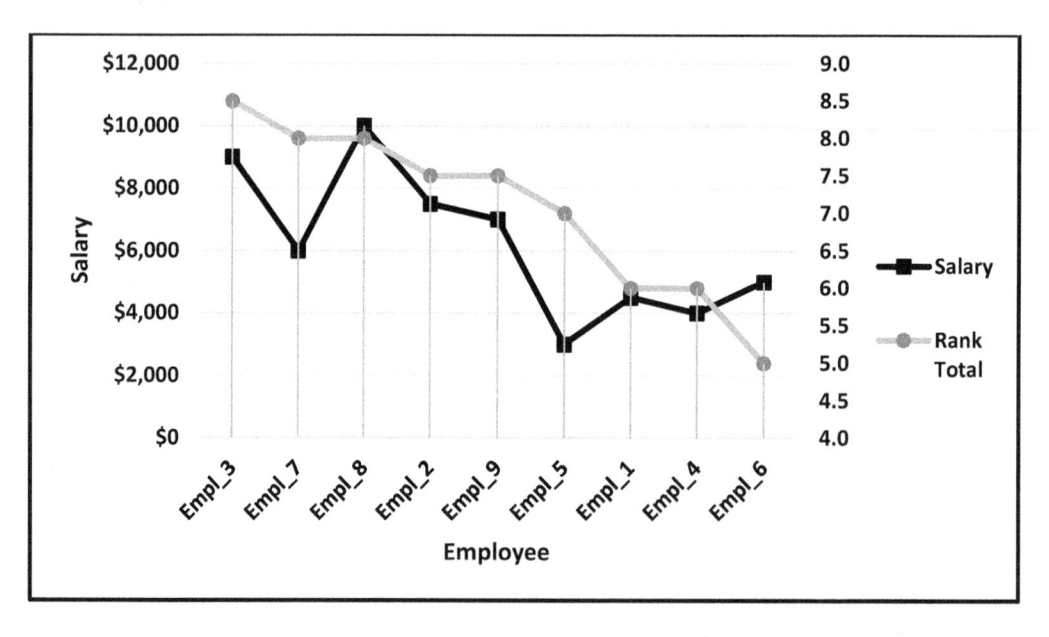

In the above graph, each employee's salary is represented on the dark line, and their ranking score is represented on the gray line. So for example, Empl_3 shows a salary of $9,000 (shown on the left axis) and a ranking score of 8.5 (shown on the right axis, off the gray line). Using a broad brush analysis, you could determine from the chart that you need to move up the salaries (higher amounts and possibly more frequently) for Employees 7 and 5, and maybe slow them down for Employees 8 and 6. This would get the salaries more "in line" so your better performers are being paid more than your lower performers.

In my experience with EDS/HP, we did not do salary cuts (except for one instance where, as a corporate-wide cost reduction measure, there was an across the board 5% temporary cut in 2009, that lasted for two years).

The salary amount you would be targeting for your people is not represented by the gray "ranking total" line which simply shows the highest to lowest ranked scores for your people. This line has nothing to do with "salary." Instead, the shape or slope of the "salary" line should somewhat match the rank total line. This would be the result if you implemented that "broad brush" salary changes mentioned in the previous paragraph. You would need to establish each person's actual salary target separately, using your established salary ranges. So assuming that you have a top-of-range salary amount, and likewise, a salary range bottom, you would need to determine where each of your people should be within that range.

It will become much clearer as soon as you start applying this tool.

6. A problem with consolidating groups in different bell curves.

"Normally," you have a few top performers, more average performers, and a few lower performers. If you happen to have a team of really good people, like a "SWAT" team of sorts, and are forced to rank them say, in quartiles for later consolidation with everyone else, your 4th quartile people in this swat team could be greater contributors compared to another team's 1st or 2nd quartile people. If you have to quickly rank your people and send it up your management chain for consolidation at the division level at corporate, without discussion, you could potentially have some exceptional performers on your team ranked much lower in the consolidation than they really should be, and where they might be unfairly penalized. In such a case you need to contact your manager and make sure to strongly explain and convey support for your people.

If it is not corrected, one consequence could be that when you submit a salary increase for one of these people, you may have to specify in what quartile they are ranked, which in fact became part of our division process, which could hurt the chance of approval or the amount allowed.

7. And if that weren't challenging enough for managers, you also need to let your people know where they are ranked.

At EDS we were required to inform our employees where they fit in the rankings – again, this was back in the 1990s. If you do rankings, you can decide how to handle this. It was important for us to inform people as to where they stood, most people wanted to know, and some would have demanded to know if we had withheld this information.

If you are going to inform people, I would highly recommend that you keep any top to bottom numerical rankings confidential if possible, and have all managers present an employee's ranking by quartile. So you might say: "you are in the top quartile," or "you are in the third quartile," or separate the groups into thirds and present it that way.

Another option would be to indicate that they are ranked in the top half or bottom half. It would be hard enough for an employee to hear that they may be in the 4th (bottom) quartile, but it might be devastating to hear that they are 29th of 30 even though they are still a good performer. Additionally, you always need to be prepared to discuss what the person can or needs to do to improve in their ranking.

Keep in mind that if you are doing a good job at managing, you do not have a single employee who is a poor performer, or who you feel should have been let go a long time ago. So when all your people are good, hard-working employees, for them to find out that they are at or near the bottom can be demoralizing. So just be sensitive to that. They need to know that you value them.

8. What needs to be done after the rankings?

Make sure you are properly rewarding your top performers. Make sure people's total compensation (salary, perks, bonuses) are commensurate with their rankings, and if not, move as aggressively as possible to rectify the inequities. And for those who are consistently at the bottom of your rankings, you need to provide guidance on what they need to do to improve or determine if they may not be a fit for your organization and take appropriate actions.

9. How can a person improve their ranking?

Here's a starting point from which you can add. Have the person ask themselves, then discuss with them:

- What were the major contributions and who were the major contributors on this project?
  - Would I put myself on this list?
  - Would my team put me on this list?
- Why would a project team want me to join them?
- Why would a project team with a tight deadline want me to join them?
- What impact have I made to my project's success?
- What have I done to go above and beyond what others have done?
- What have I done to be more productive in getting needed work done?
- What have I done to position myself to have the skills that the company will be needing?

10. Pay and new opportunities based on performance, related to gender.

In my experience with EDS, throughout my 32+ year career, there was never any discussion or concerns raised related to gender inequality, whether it be on pay for performance or on any other matter. There was no special attention or effort to make sure that our female employees were fairly considered for new opportunities, or for leadership positions, or for bonuses and salary increases. We never ran stats to make sure that we were being fair and equitable. Our focus was always on who is bringing the most value, who is contributing the most, who is getting the best and most consistent results, and who would be the best person for any new opportunities. Here are some statistics on my SoCal SE Center in 1999, not including the Satellite Center staff of 20 since I did not have their salary info readily available – in-other-words I couldn't find it.

Account staff (94 total, not including the satellite center):

- Total non-management staff : 85
    - 35%   Female
    - 65%   Male
- Management Team: 9
    - 44%   Female
    - 56%   Male
- Of the top 15% highest paid employees:
    - 38%   Female
    - 62%   Male
- Top 15% highest paid with management team added:
    - 41%   Female
    - 59%   Male

This appears to show that female employees were fairly represented among the highest paid people, relative to their percentage of the overall staff, if not slightly better.

It also shows that my management team was fairly represented relative to gender. Then when the management team is added to the highest paid salary group, the female percentage ticks up a little higher.

It's important to note that I had never done this type of a "gender" analysis until writing this book. With gender pay and opportunity inequities being a real-world global problem, I wanted to see how we might have stacked up back when I had a large organization in the 1990's and 2000. The stats above are just how the chips fell, by our management team's focus on paying for performance and results, and opportunities going to the best person for the job. This is simply how we learned to do things from our EDS managers who mentored us. I also believe that this is simply the result of having a company culture with solid ethical principles at its foundation.

The following has nothing to do with rankings and compensation but since I was running some account stats, here are a few more on my organization's staff diversity at the SoCal SE Center, which again, I had never done before writing this book. I believe this is very typical of the ethnic diversity in the IT industry to today.

- 65% Caucasian
- 24% Asian
- 5% Hispanic
- 3% African American
- 3% Middle Eastern

Dealing with Complaints and Discontent

1. Complainers.

I'm sure it's common in many work environments to have a range of people from the strong company and team supporters, to those who are constant complainers. As a manager with a larger team of people, it's probably inevitable that you'll have at least one person who might fall into the category of "complainers."

I've had employees who were generally good and productive employees, but who were also frequent complainers. Note that any concerns or complaints raised regarding illegal, unethical, unprofessional, or unfair actions and behaviors need to be heeded and dealt with promptly. So I'm not talking about things in the vein of unsafe working conditions or unfair treatment of employees or "union busting." You also don't want to be on the evening news trying to explain why you allowed such bad behavior to take place in your office either.

But then you'll also see complaints on things that might be more in line with personal preferences or one person's perception of unfairness, or why can't we get better cubicle chairs, and the list goes on and on.

And this is over and above an annual employee survey that we conducted, where people could provide input anonymously, and with management dedicating time to prioritize concerns raised, taking actions to address, and then reporting on the results.

Some key points are:
1. You must always promptly address illegal, unethical, and other bad behavior,
2. Provide an avenue for employees to voice their concerns or to offer recommendations for improvement, in a safe (non-threatening) environment, and
3. Management needs to budget time to be able to address concerns, consider ideas for improvement, and implement the best ideas.

If you don't do these things, you lose credibility among your employees and worse; you will limit the overall and long-term health and productivity improvement of your organization.

With that said, do not let constant complainers monopolize a significant amount of your time. A complainer can be a magnet for other complainers, can become a spokesperson for complainers, and can even encourage more complainers.

You'll always have constraints on money and time. You are operating against a budget, so you don't have the option to spend on upgrades to satisfy each request, and you don't have the time and resources to chase down every complaint. You'll also find that if you apply a fix for one complaint, that fix will cause problems for others. Then, of course, you have the entire business to run, project issues to address, customers to satisfy, and corporate requirements and targets to hit.

2. Keep complainers in perspective.

You'll probably always find a few people who although do good work, have the need to complain about the workplace or to criticize management. For whatever reason, some people seem to have a high degree of distrust for management, believe that things are being poorly run, or maybe simply have a low tolerance for what they consider distractions and annoyances, and are consistently unhappy at work. They would somehow have a list of complaints after a day at Disneyland. Others seem to enjoy the attention they receive when they can find and point out problems in the workplace.

As stated above, as a leader, you always have to be on the look-out for problem areas, inefficiencies, and inequities, so you can appropriately take action to address these.

But you will also get frustrated sometimes (can you tell?) at the constant grousing and complaining by a very few. The thing is, these complainers are among your good performers, so except for their complaining, they do good work.

But if you allow it, chronic complainers can command an exorbitant amount of your time, emotional energy, and even organizational resources.

Some complainers can be bottomless pits. When you think you've addressed one of their problems, they will find another. They are generally a loud negative voice in a group where 95% of the others are fine with their work and the work environment. (Now if the percentages are such that you have a high amount of the dissatisfied, then you have long ignored problems in your workplace.)

Do not take the time and energy that you could and should spend to recognize, reward, and advance the opportunities for the rest of your good employees. Give more attention to those who make a positive impact on your organization, and don't waste it on "high maintenance" chronic complainers.

If a person consistently complains or is unhappy, you and they, need to discuss and determine if he/she is a long-term match for the work environment, team, organization, or company. I say this because, in my experience, complainers don't change. Consider this: how many people in your organization or team who consistently have a good positive attitude, have you ever seen change to having a bad attitude? Few to none would be my guess.

So again, after doing your due diligence to address valid concerns, focus more of your time on your good productive people. And this may not be easy because complainers can demand and command a great deal of attention. You could be criticized for ignoring employee concerns, for example.

They could escalate a concern to your manager and complain about your inaction. So no quick fixes or easy answers on this. Just spend less time and energy on your complainers.

3. Be upfront.

If an employee who is a constant complainer is also your poorest performer, and they are negatively impacting morale or impeding the productivity of others, then you need to look at replacing this person. If a complainer is a good performer, but you feel the person's complaint or issue ranks low on your "what's important" list, then be upfront. Never ignore or blow anyone off. You could say something like, "I understand that this is important to you but to be honest, when I look at our list of priorities for this organization, and with our resource constraints, I could not place your concern on that list. I hope you can accept that at this point, I don't intend to take any action on this. I need to focus on matters that are more pressing, and that will have a bigger organizational impact."

4. Never immediately side with or encourage someone who has a complaint about someone else – you must hear both sides.

Making a decision, or taking a position, based on hearing only one side of the story, no matter how obvious or compelling it may appear, would not be fair, and would be again, like crossing the street after looking in only one direction. From early EDS Leadership training, we learned that when you have arguments of competing views, don't go back and forth hearing each person's side individually and try to sort things out by yourself. Instead, "get all the liars in one room" – from Perot's leadership training. Have a sit-down with them in a conference room or your office, or on a conference call if necessary, and hash it out directly. If one or both are reluctant to face each other, well, you are the manager and you establish the requirements.

This will be the fastest and most effective way to get the concerns out into the open, to help come to a resolution, which could ultimately turn out to be, "we agree to disagree."

5. A tip on how not to respond if you think you've been criticized.

Suppose someone tells you that they heard Pat say that you did a lousy job on a project. You then respond in anger with, "well, he's a jerk, and I never liked working with him anyway." You may have said this in anger, but probably mostly hurt, and it may or may not have been how you actually felt about him. Then it turns out that Pat never said that, or he was referring to someone else, or maybe it was misinterpreted, or whatever. A big problem now right?! A more prudent response might have been, "really, we've worked on a lot of projects together so I'll need to hear that from him myself." You can then leave it at that, or verify if necessary.

6. Beware of the few who always tend to talk behind people's back.

I touched upon this earlier but it's worth mentioning again. A few people seem to enjoy the reaction they get when criticizing or making fun of others. Keep in mind that if they are telling you unflattering things about others, they are likely telling others unflattering things about you. It's unprofessional so don't engage in this type of unproductive back-biting. If someone engages you with such a comment, you could, 1) simply offer a polite smile, but no other response and continue with what you were doing, 2) change the subject, or 3) offer no reaction/ignore it and walk away.

They will get the message that you are not an open ear for such comments or behavior, and that you won't be jumping in to contribute to it.

7. Be aware of people who often criticize others.

This type of criticism can be disheartening and demoralizing to those being criticized, and who will often hear this through the grapevine. Sometimes there are people who generally don't take on tough or risky challenges, but who are quick to criticize those who do. They tend to hide in a safe place, stick to what they do well, and lob criticisms to those who are trying to stretch themselves or trying to implement any kind of change in the workplace. I've never found these people to be among the top performers. I've seen people hesitate from taking opportunities due to the fear of being criticized by a few people. It's your responsibility to ensure that you have a supportive work environment where people feel that they can take risks to better themselves and the team.

This is what allows people to spread their wings. Otherwise, your organization will not be firing on all cylinders.

8. Some people believe that the company always owes them, because of their years of loyalty.

I remember hearing some complaints along these lines from someone earlier in my career, and bringing it up to my manager at the time who had been with EDS for 25 years. I remember him adamantly pointing out that "yes, we value their contributions and loyalty, but don't forget that they have always received a paycheck, it was always on time, and they always had good company benefits: Medical, Dental, 401K, training, career opportunities, etc. It goes both ways!" So don't allow employees to try to leverage their years of service and loyalty to the company to get something they want, as though you owe it to them.

If you've done a good job taking care of your employees as a manager or business owner, then you may have to remind them that it's been a two-way street. In return for their years of service, you've helped to take care of them, which has allowed them to take care of their families. So as a manager, make sure you do your level best to care for your employees.

9. Soliciting input on employee concerns.

Getting employee input, like an annual "voice of the employee" or "voice of the workforce," is a good way to identify, and determine how critical and widespread concerns might be. A word of advice: be careful about setting expectations on your ability to resolve concerns and how long it might take because you won't have unlimited resources to research the problems, identify the root causes, come up with alternative solutions and process fixes, then implement corrective actions. On certain things, you may need to first get approval from upper management at corporate as well. Then after corrective actions are implemented, you'll need to track and follow up to ensure it is working or determine if any tweaking is necessary, which in themselves require resources.

Give particular consideration to quick turn-around low hanging fruit.

Never ask your people for an open-ended list of "problems or issues" that they feel need to be addressed and fixed. You should instead do the following:

- Ask for people's top 3 to 5 concerns.
- Compile and consolidate those lists of concerns. Hopefully, you won't have like 350 of them, then send it out to the entire staff and ask people to put a value next to their top concerns, with a limitation that the total score

can't exceed say 10. So they might put a 5 next to their biggest concern, a 3 next to the second worst, and a 2 next to the third, where the three items add up to 10. This way, you get the concerns that are most important to them.

- Consolidate these and their scores. The biggest concerns will float to the top, then select say, the top 5 max, to take improvement actions.

This way, you avoid producing a huge wish list of 100 things that "would make things a whole lot better around here," some of which may not be that critical or even important to many people. By requiring this type of weighting to the concerns, you can get a more quantitative assessment of the biggest concerns among your team, get the list down to the top 3 to 5, then communicate this final list to your employees and take actions to address. Otherwise, you'll likely end up with a laundry list of items, with only a few that you could reasonably address due to limited time and resources.

Not Funny – A Little Disrespectful

There were a couple of times in my management career where some people didn't seem to take me seriously as a manager. This would probably never happen if you have a more commanding or aggressive/assertive Type A personality, but if you don't, like me, this could happen to you.

It could start with a few people joking around a little too much, or making fun of what you said in a playful way – but then it starts going a little over the line, to the point where maybe you are becoming the brunt of some jokes. Now I always had a good sense of humor and always tried to have fun with everyone, but there's a limit to that when you're the manager, and if you allow a few people to take it over the line, it can expand to others doing the same. So you have to nip that in the bud. This can be a double-edged sword, however, because if you don't handle this properly, you could be seen as someone who is demanding respect because of your position of authority.

But regardless, maintaining that line is more important.

There was this one person who was actually a customer of ours, who used to kind of chuckle when we discussed things and when I would make a point in our discussions. I noticed it happening a few times and didn't think much of it at first, but I then started to get a little concerned that this was becoming a common response from him, where I was getting a sense that he was not taking me seriously. When he did this again, where he kind of chuckled at a comment that I made regarding a project, I finally asked him, in a calm but firm demeanor, "is there something I'm saying that you're finding amusing?" After a pause, and I was going to wait as long as it took, he came back with a "no, no, sorry, I get what you're saying," he never did that again, and we continued with a good relationship like it never happened.

In another situation, there were two female employees, one more at a senior level. For some reason, when the two were together talking, and I would come by, they would make some comment or light-hearted joke about me, intending for the three of us to laugh. They knew that I had a good sense of humor. Now again, it was not anything crass or demeaning, but it was becoming every time like a "habit," and no one wants to be the brunt of jokes all the time, even if intended to be good natured. So when it happened again, I finally pointed out "hey, this is becoming not so funny." They said, oh, OK, and seemed to be fine with it but I could tell they didn't appreciate being told that, even though I was their manager. But as uncomfortable as it was, I had to put a stop to it.

No matter how insignificant, you can't allow this kind of habitual joking about you as the manager, or as the head of the organization. It's disrespectful.

> *This situation actually reminded me, however, that I had been guilty of this as well. During my second year in college, a surfing friend of mine and I would be sitting in the campus cafeteria for lunch, and every time this good-natured friend of ours who was younger and a gremmy (surfing beginner) came in with the place full of students, we'd yell out as he approached us "ehhh, surfa!" and the three of us would laugh. We did that to him every time, and it became a habit for us until he finally asked us one day if we could not say that anymore because it was starting to make him look and feel bad. We realized then that this really was not a cool thing to do, because without thinking, we were making fun of him, and in front of a lot of other people, so we told him how sorry we were and we never did it again.*

The lesson here is to never do this to a co-worker and especially not to your manager, consciously or unconsciously.

As the Head of a Business, You Establish the Work Environment and Culture

1. **When you are the head of a business or organization, the buck stops with you period.**

There is no question, no doubts, and no confusion on who is to blame if things go wrong. "Oh, I thought Curtis, the Operations Manager, was handling that" won't fly, and even if you had given Curtis that responsibility, Curtis is your employee, so it's still your responsibility.

2. **As the owner or head of a business or organization, you establish the business and operational culture and how you are perceived by your customers.**

This section focusses on you as the manager of your own business, or office, or facility. This topic has more to do with you being responsible for the work environment – the day-to-day workings within your office, where you may have to exert more influence and even control on how things are done.

As an example, when you manage a team or organization within a larger office, you are not necessarily responsible for how the phones are answered, or how your customers or visitors are greeted at the reception desk, or have to deal with people who dress a little too casually, etc.

When you are responsible for the entire office, everything becomes a reflection on you as the head of the office and your expectations as the manager. This is where the EDS leadership phrase "you get what you tolerate," becomes significantly magnified. If you do not personally correct rude behavior in the workplace, for example, you are indirectly encouraging it, and there will be more instances of this behavior.

If you don't point out to people that they are over the line relative to the dress code, say goodbye to your dress code. Similarly, if you don't recognize and pat people on the back for good performance and behaviors, you are missing golden opportunities to encourage and promote the type of environment that you may truly desire for your business, for your employees, and for your customers.

3. Everything reflects on you as the manager.

Make no mistake, the behaviors and actions of your employees, and the positive or negative perception of your business or organization by your customers is a reflection on you, the owner or "person in charge." To stop any unwanted or unprofessional behavior and actions of your employees, you need the mettle to confront and personally correct them. You'll get undesirable behaviors and actions that you exhibit yourself, and therefore encourage, consciously or unconsciously.

> *I once was on a TDY assignment at an EDS office that was within a much larger customer facility. Prior to arriving there, I had heard that the manager in charge tended to get a little hot under the collar at times. I got a feel for that a couple of times while sitting in my temporary cube when I could hear him raising his voice in anger to some people in his office, although I couldn't see who was in there. That was my first and only time I ever experienced this in EDS.*
>
> *One evening, a younger colleague and I went into the office to work on our project. Going into the office in the evening was not a big deal because we had security access into the customer's facility, and then separately into the EDS offices, so besides having pre-authorized evening access, our IDs were being recorded, and employees did that all the time.*
>
> *We completed our work and were heading out when we heard someone else working down another aisle, so we went by to say hello, and also, out of courtesy, to let the person know who we were since it was in the evening, and particularly if it happened to be a female co-worker.*
>
> *We recognized the person, and he had seen us before, so we said hello, but before we could get another word in, for some reason, he went on a rant, asking why we were there, that we were visitors so we shouldn't be there, and on and on. I said OK, good night, and we left. Now if we had been a real security risk, he would have followed protocol which would*

*have been to immediately alert security, but that certainly wasn't the issue. He wanted to show us who was in charge, and he was clearly proud of it. As we walked out my colleague was in shock. I told him, "**that**, was a reflection of his manager." It was like a light bulb went on for him and he turned to me and said: "you're right!"*

Bear with me as I use another example on establishing an office or organizational culture. This one is from my Hilo Boys' Club days.

I had been a member since I was seven years old, all the way through Intermediate School. The Director the entire time was Shell Blanchet, who was my baseball and football coach for many years, and another valuable mentor. The point I'm getting to here is that I remember that the Boys' Club facility, the games area with pool tables, ping pong tables, etc., and also the library, wood shop, locker rooms, and huge gym, were always clean and spotless.

Although full of us young mischievous kids, there were no scratches on the walls, no markings in the toilets, no holes or intentional damaging of any kind, anywhere. This was no doubt, due to the leadership of Director Shell, and his firmness to hold everyone accountable for our behavior. If someone made a scratch or markings on anything, and the culprit could not be identified, Shell, and he wanted everyone to call him that, not Mr. Blanchet, would shut down the entire games room for a day or two or more, depending on the severity of the scratches. If markings or some intentional damage were found in the locker room, he would shut down the gym with multiple basketball courts, a trampoline, gymnastics equipment, etc., with equal severity. All of us would be totally bummed. In all of my 7 or 8 years at the Boys' Club, I can count on one hand how many times areas were shut down. All the kids self-policed the place.

There was no graffiti anywhere, no scratching or writings in the bathroom stalls, no holes in the walls, nothing. Under Shell's leadership, the place was immaculate.

In contrast, I was also a member of the YMCA when I was in Intermediate and High School, and benefited from the move and upgrade from a broken down old building, into a brand new beautiful facility. It was maybe only 1/3rd the size of the Boy's Club but very nice. Now the members here were older, intermediate and high school-aged teens, but I was shocked to see how little things at the facility slowly got damaged over time, and intentionally by people. Room number signs were getting marked up, ceramic signs were chipped off, and writings were left in the toilet stalls.

It wasn't until many years later that I realized that bottom line, how an office looks and how people behave, all comes down to the head of that office or company or facility. You need to establish your expectations and be willing to personally hold people to them. It's important to note that this does not mean that this YMCA director was a poor director because that would be far from the truth. This person had a major positive influence on many people's lives, including my own.

But this leader did not know how to hold people accountable for certain behaviors, and the overall appearance of the facility reflected this.

The point is that when you walk into a place of business, a store, or an office, its look and feel, and how you are treated, will be a reflection of the owner, or the person who manages that business, or store, or office.

If the person at the top is always a nice person and would never be rude to anyone, but people in his front office are unfriendly to customers and visitors, he is responsible for allowing this to occur. He either doesn't care, or doesn't have the nerve to confront his employees and get them to change their behaviors, so they probably also consider him a push-over.

The unfriendly behavior by his staff may not be a reflection of him the person, but it is definitely a reflection of him as the owner, or manager, or leader.

4. Here are some things that I did to maintain a professional work environment.

I realize that things like the dress standards and work culture have changed significantly over my 32 plus years with the company, so take this into consideration as you read on. Earlier, I described how strict EDS' dress code was back when I started in the early 1980s. Much has changed but what hasn't changed is that there are always some company and office standards or expectations by which people need to abide. So there will always

Management Responsibilities

be instances where the standards will be crossed, and it will always be difficult for you to have to confront people to make sure this is corrected.

Here are some examples, and keep in mind that in these, I tried to be firm but not angry or demanding. Also, note that none are employee performance related.

- Twice I had to send people home to change because they came into the office inappropriately dressed. One was a new receptionist who one day wore a dress that was a little more revealing than was acceptable for our corporate culture.

- I coached someone, after a meeting, and after everyone had left, to please not joke around in the back of the conference room while the meeting was going on – even though he was being discreet, it was important to have everyone's full attention.

- I asked a few people to please not walk around the office with a toothpick sticking out of their mouth. This might seem awfully picky but keep in mind that this was at a time when we were all dressed in suits. However, when I think about it, if I had my own business office today, I still would not allow this. Go figure – too old school I guess.

- I asked someone not to wear his hat in the office, but handled it poorly. This was during the time when "casual days" were starting to become more frequent, like every Fridays, or when there was a big project success. When this person came to the office wearing a hat, I knew I had to nip that in the bud, but the person wearing it was one of our top performers and I struggled with the thought of having to approach him at his cube to bring it up. I finally got up the nerve to walk over there, but when I got there, I started chitchatting about what he was working on. I finally brought up the issue and asked him to please not wear the hat in the office, where he complied, and it appeared to be no big deal. But I felt lousy about it for a long time because I was there beating around the bush with a hidden agenda, until I could build up my courage to get to the point. I never did that beat-around-the-bush thing again.

- Several times when I noticed that our facility restroom urinals had that odor like they were not properly cleaned, I immediately contacted the property management office to get this corrected. Facilities got the message because this happened maybe only one other time in the years that we were in this particular office building – or maybe others on my staff took action. I would do the same if we ran out of paper, soap, etc. I asked a couple of my female managers to please do the same if anything was awry in the women's restroom. I simply wanted to make sure that my team and any visitors had a neat, clean, and professional office in which to work.

- I had to ask someone organizing an office event not to refer to the luncheon as having "free food" in the invitation that went out to the office. To me, this reference somehow lowered the value of the event. Of course, in the grand scheme of things, this might sound extremely petty, but this is how you put your fingerprints on your business – it gets down to some of your personal preferences and choices on how to maintain your office or business culture and professionalism. Now if I had been overly petty with these and other things that I did, I definitely would have heard about it because our employees were not shy, and we always got management feedback that could also be anonymous. But the staff was always very professional, and I know they appreciated maintaining a highly professional workplace.

Although it can be extremely difficult to have to point out some unpleasant things to your people, it is extremely rewarding to see that at your office, people by far, treat one another courteously and respectfully, visitors consistently praise your staff for their friendliness and helpfulness, and the office is clean, well kept, and a very professional environment. It's important to point out that I did not come into this organization as its manager and have to fix a mess. I came in and worked hard to ensure that I maintained the high standards and professionalism that had already been established by my EDS predecessors who were also great mentors.

CHAPTER 5:
PROJECT MANAGEMENT

Context

The discussions in this chapter relate to some key aspects and also a broader perspective of Project Management – like making sure you understand the scope and requirements, coordination and communication with the team, and ensuring that your people are on track and are meeting expectations.

This does not necessarily mean that you have to be designated as a Project Manager, or that you have the title as one. Even as an individual performer, you'll be tasked with official or unofficial "projects" of all sizes.

When I was a supervisor, well before I was officially a PM, I was tasked with a multitude of "assignments" that ranged from small to large and complex projects. As an example, I was tasked with the site move of our entire SE Center offices from Anaheim to Orange, CA. This represented coordinating the buildout at the new site, the move of every physical piece of equipment and furniture, the setup of the infrastructure, security system, networking, and communications gear, and every little detail until people were in their new cubes and offices and it was business as usual.

Then as a manager, still not a PM, years later, along with my other responsibilities, I was assigned to coordinate the move from Orange to Cypress, CA.

I had never thought of these as "projects" at the time, but that's what they were.

You don't need to be a Project Manager to get some valuable lessons learned from what I discuss in this chapter. This, however, will not cover the nuts and bolts of Project Management. For that, I highly recommend referencing the Project Management Institute (PMI), and their Project Management Professional (PMP) certification program (also Agile/ScrumMaster). I am PMP credentialed, but as you might expect from my earlier writings in the book, it took me not one, but two attempts to pass the PMP exam, where I failed miserably in my first attempt. It is an extremely challenging and let me say grueling undertaking.

But if your job is primarily focused on managing projects or activities, this effort to prepare and get PMP certified will give you invaluable knowledge, tools, and techniques that you will be

Project Management 133

able to apply immediately. It will improve your results, and help you avoid some terrible pitfalls. It will also increase your credibility and standing as a PM in the marketplace.

The topics I discuss here should give you valuable tips on project management to add to what is generally covered in the PMI's formal PMP study program.

1. Manager vs. Project Manager

I once read an article about someone being criticized for being "only" a Project Manager, and not a "real" Manager. Here are some of my thoughts on this since I've had many years of people and organizational management, as well as project management experience (and with a PMP).

- Very simply and in general, as a PM, I most often had a matrixed team, people assigned to me as opposed to reporting directly to me, and with having a primary mission – to complete a project by a planned deadline. This is simply stated, but the PM role is immensely more challenging and difficult than this statement might lead you to believe, and I discuss more of this in this chapter.

- As a general "manager" in contrast, I had an organization/team where I was responsible for work assignments, performance reviews, compensation and recognition, career development, coaching and mentoring, etc. I also had financials responsibility like budgeting, profit and loss (P&L) accountability, salary administration, facilities management, etc.

- So the "manager" role is broader in the business and administrative areas.

- You could not take a successful PM, put them in charge of an organization, and expect them to quickly fulfill all the business, administrative, and people responsibilities of a general manager.

- A Project Manager, on the other hand, generally has a narrower area of focus, and requires a broader/deeper set of skills in the PM disciplines including managing project scope, resourcing and skill matching, laying out the project timeline, costing the project, quality management, evaluating risks and planning for contingencies, monitoring and controlling the project, etc. It also requires experience in the use of PM software tools where for me, they were Microsoft's Project Professional and HP's Project Portfolio Management (PPM). I also found that as a PM, deadlines and people accountability had to be monitored very closely, and addressed more frequently. You could not take your eyes off the ball with, in particular, the project deliverables, all the tightly integrated downstream components, and the schedule.

- As a general manager, I always had a number of people with whom I could delegate different responsibilities or to handle a crisis of some kind.

- As a PM, you are always on point for everything. Anything that comes up on the project that needs to be addressed or fixed, from little details to potential major project complications become your responsibility to run to the ground. If you have to do a major change to your schedule, for example, you'll need to bring all your project management skills and experience to bear. You would definitely not have time to do salary increase write-ups, or research and conduct performance reviews, or to organize this year's "voice of the worker" program for the organization.

- So likewise, you could not just take a successful general manager, put them in the role of a PM for a challenging project, and expect them to be immediately successful.

- Having been a manager running a small piece of EDS' business, having skilled and experienced Project Managers was absolutely critical to our success.

- Then to counter the original point above, PMs could also say, and rightfully so, "oh, those folks are 'only' managers, they're not 'real' Project Managers!"

- They both have different roles, requiring different skills, and fill different very impactful needs.

- One common, very important, and often very difficult requirement for both though, is having to personally hold people accountable to their commitments and to your expectations.

2. The PM is always on point.

As the Project Manager, expect that people will always point to you if anything needs to get done. When any problem or issue comes up related to your project, and I mean any and all, expect customers and stakeholders to say "go talk to the PM to take care of it" or "go ask the PM what the heck is going on!" If something didn't get done that was supposed to get done, make no mistake, it won't matter who dropped the ball, it is ultimately your responsibility, and you are the one who will get the calls and have to provide answers. So you need to make sure that you track and stay on top of everything and everyone, even if you have sub-teams with leaders.

Be prepared to solve problem after problem, and take care of surprise after surprise, as much as you try to keep up and stay ahead of everything.

For certain problems that come up, you may not have the expertise nor authority to resolve the issue, so you'll have to track down the resource with the specialized skills that you need. Ultimately, you may need to escalate, starting with your manager, or contact the head of the group from whom you need assistance (engineering, networking, testing, etc.).

After your polite request doesn't work, you'll have to use as much leverage as you can muster. You might insist that, say, if you can't get the resource you need, you won't be able to meet the project deadline, and you'll need to delay this deliverable to the customer by a week, or whatever the consequence may be. The amount of assistance you get will generally be directly proportional to the priority and visibility of your project.

There are many and bigger risks for a PM taking on a high priority project, but this is one of the up-sides – you can usually get whatever you need when the going gets rough if some high-level manager's head might roll because your project was delayed or failed.

3. Make sure you have firm requirements before you offer any delivery dates.

Never buckle to pressure and give a project schedule before you know the requirements and key dependencies. You can count on being pressured for this after being given "rough" requirements from time to time as a PM. If you do, it will be like launching through a red light because the guy behind you starts blasting his horn. "How can I give you a schedule, even a rough estimate, when I'm still waiting for the final requirements?!"

If you prematurely give even a "rough" delivery date, you can probably bet that it will somehow get out to all your customers, and it will become the "expected" delivery date. So make sure any dates you provide, rough or otherwise, are experienced based, and with a level of confidence in your understanding of the requirements and dependencies. In other words, make sure you have a clear enough view of what's ahead, and that you're not trying to make things out while looking through thick fog.

You'll be held accountable for any dates you throw out, as you should be.

4. Double-check dates or timelines that are provided to you.

Whenever you are talking about project delivery dates with your team and the customer, make sure everyone on your team is in sync on what dates are being provided to the customer. I've held cross-functional team meetings which included the customer where on one particular project, a functional group representative said that the required change would be completed in two days, so the customer believed and communicated to their counterparts that the delay would only be for two days. However, upon verification after the meeting, I learned that the two days were only for the engineering work to be done, but it still needed several levels of reviews and approvals, as well as lab testing before the change could be implemented, which doubled the duration.

So the lesson is if you are working in unfamiliar territory and with various groups, which will likely be very common, make sure you press functional teams for more details on the timelines they provide for their deliverables. Also, keep in mind that in time-sensitive situations, people are under pressure to deliver sooner/faster – "how long will you take?", "can you get it done sooner?", "I'll talk to your manager so you can drop everything else and work exclusively on this!" Under such conditions, they may provide over-aggressive (unrealistic) time frames to try to please you, or the customer, or the people in the room, so they are not seen as the "bad guy."

Be aware that, unless you have confidence in people based on track record, you can't simply go on anything that they provide to you. You have to do your due diligence, starting with some probing questions.

5. Technical experience.

You will probably have to accept the fact that you'll often not have solid technical experience in the various areas that your projects will cover. In many of the projects that I managed, I did not have a firm understanding or grasp of the underlying technology. In some, it was minimal to none. In almost all of the projects that I managed, I had to depend upon a few senior or expert level technical people.

Many of these people were very, very smart and highly experienced in their disciplines, but if you get people like this, don't be immediately intimidated as I had been. You'll likely find that most of them do not have the skills nor the desire, to do your job. They do not want to plan, or coordinate, or have to chase down every potential problem, or to be the one to hold people accountable for their deliverables on a project.

In other words, most of them will love the fact that **you** have to handle all the sh*t that comes up on the project. They'll appreciate the job and responsibilities that you've taken on.

It will also be your responsibility as the PM, to get all these "smart and experienced people" together to determine what needs to get done, and the best way to get it done. They'll also need to help you determine who you're going to need or who you better get, and how long it's going to take. Then plot the course and move forward, resolve any issues to keep the project on track, hold people accountable, and to take it over the goal line.

Do not commit to doing a project without having key people with the required expertise assigned to it. Similarly, you would not commit to complete the building of a house by a certain date, without the assurance of having access to an electrician, plumber, etc.

If you are going in cold, you'll need to depend on your manager and sponsors to ensure that you are covered with the people you are going to need for your project.

6. Project teams.

As a project manager, you'll likely get people assigned to your project from different functional areas, where each employee reports directly to their functional area manager but is on "loan" to you for the project. Your team then forms a cross-functional or matrixed team that exists for the life of the project. There are unique challenges in managing a project and holding people accountable for their project commitments when they are assigned to your project, but do not formally report to you.

An employee's "real" manager has significantly more authority and influence over their employees because they are responsible for their career development, rewards and recognition, compensation, promotions, etc. As a PM, you generally do not have that same level of influence on your project team members.

The challenges are compounded when your team is made up of people who are geographically dispersed, where they might be in other offices across the city, in other states, or countries.

7. Accountability on matrixed project teams.

I've found that with matrixed teams, particularly when they are geographically dispersed, there's an increased chance that you may have to closely monitor certain individuals to ensure that they meet their project commitments, at least initially.

I've learned that you can't assume that everyone will complete their tasks and do all the things expected of them. If you have an individual that misses a deadline, carefully assess what the cause may be. Does the person not have adequate experience, did they misunderstand the requirements, or do you need to pair someone up with this person temporarily? Take whatever measures are necessary, but you'll need to focus more attention on this individual. If meeting their dates continues to be questionable, ask for updates more frequently. Start requiring the person to proactively inform you when their taskings are done with a call or an email.

Mark your calendar and if you don't hear anything when expected, you need to promptly pick up the phone and make a call to that person to confirm if they've completed their taskings one way or the other. Another option might be to acquire the person's commitment date in writing.

If you can't get the person to send you a commitment (I've had people try to ignore me); for starters, you could send the person an email asking him/her to confirm that he/she will complete the work by a certain date and make sure that you get a confirmation reply. This may help ensure that the job gets done, and you also send a message that they need to keep to their commitments because you will consistently follow up if you don't hear back.

Hopefully, the person will start to demonstrate a greater sense of urgency in keeping you apprised, and if so, you can start loosening up. If they don't, see further below.

In addition, you could call or meet with the individual to confirm their commitment date. It's critical that you both understand that the commitment is due 'by when,' with a specific date and time. If the deadline is July 10th, well does that mean you expect it by noon of July 10, or does the person think that he/she has until close-of-business on the 10th, and is it by 12 noon Eastern Time or Pacific Time? Believe me, these have been issues I've had to deal with when working with teams across the country. And it's not necessarily because people are trying to get away with anything, it may be related to what they are accustomed to and with whom they usually work. So as the lead, you have to make sure everyone is on the same page on expectations.

Whenever it becomes clear that there is a performance problem, you'll need to address it right away. Since on a matrixed team, this person reports to another manager, you may first need to bring this up with your own manager. If you are a higher level PM, you may be able to address it with that person's manager directly. If talking to the person's manager gets no results, then you definitely need to take it to your manager so they can have a manager-to-manager discussion. I have gone so far as to take an issue up to an individual's manager's manager due to inaction.

Whenever you take an issue up the chain to get addressed, you always need to have done your homework on the problem and have all the background information, dates, and facts to back up your concerns. Make sure that you can answer any questions on this issue from your manager or the individual's manager, which means that you have given careful thought to what you may be asked about the matter. In my experience, the persons in question generally get a fire lit under them, and we no longer have a problem, or the person is ultimately replaced.

All of this requires a lot of extra time and work, and causes frustration but also gets a lot worse the longer you wait to take action.

You should get to the point where your expectations are established throughout the project team, and you can completely trust that everyone will be on top of things. Again, it's a balancing act because you need to be firm, but you don't want to be demanding and threatening. As the PM, you need people to feel safe to let you know if there are issues and if they're having difficulties and may need some assistance. When everyone understands the expectations and always gets done what they need to get done and on time, then things run more smoothly, and with significantly less stress.

> *One of the people who helped to train me when I joined the PM group, and who became a good friend and colleague, is a retired US Marine Corps Colonel. He was way up there in the PM experience ranks so was a frequent go-to person for me as we supported the Navy, and where he was always extremely generous with his time, as long as I was on the ball. On a few occasions, he sat in on my meetings to offer advice and guidance as a subject matter expert. After two of the meetings, on separate occasions, he told me "Norm, you're too nice." I laughed a bit, but he did not, both times. He was among the top PMs, with his own style, so there you go, different styles and strokes for different folks.*

To add some historical context, earlier in my career, in the 1980s and early 1990s, projects running "smoothly and with less stress" in EDS were generally the exception rather than the rule. But this was not because we lacked good people. First, it seemed like overnight, General Motors became our owner and primary customer, and all of GM's data processing (DP) became EDS' responsibility, which put huge demands on the company. GM's DP personnel also moved to EDS.

But in addition to the impact due to this huge growth, in our Information Technology (IT) line of business, advances in technology, acute competitive pressures, ever-increasing customer and industry demands to improve levels of service, forced us to stretch to our limits. Then add to this the financial pressures for contract deliverables, most significantly due to overly aggressive sales deals (there was a huge priority to diversify and expand our non-GM business), and the result was exhaustive "death marches," with projects requiring 12 to 14+ hour days, weekend work, some all-nighters, many weeks to many months at a time. I was on a number of them, and it was often doing some kind of IT work that we had never done before.

For many who had been with the company during that time, it certainly felt like the EDS commercial "Airplane" that came out years later in 2000, where it was about building an aircraft while it was in the air.

8. Peer pressure to motivate.

On a matrixed team, a method to exert influence indirectly, meaning without having to pressure people directly with a meeting or a phone call, is to set up something like a dashboard. If people are consistently late with things, especially if they don't think they are important, like their timesheets (critical with government contract work), or status reports, etc., post a public list of people and a chart, by day or week, showing who was on time and who was late. Be judicious of course. At first, maybe some people won't care that they show up late. They might think "Why are they measuring this?" or "What's the big deal?" But after there are a few columns of history, and everyone is on time except for only one or two people who consistently show up late, peer pressure can start making an impact.

This was used to compare different EDS accounts at the management level on such things as "which accounts showed 100% on-time Performance Reviews", and "which accounts showed zero (0) late Time Sheets". So even things that might seem non-critical to business operations, when measured and put on a dashboard with your peers, will escalate in priority, big time.

You won't want to be the only one in noncompliance. Something to add to your toolbox.

9. Post-meeting actions summary.

After every project meeting, make absolutely sure that everyone clearly understands what needs to be done, the next steps, who needs to follow up on or complete what, when it's due, etc. It's essential that you summarize and review with the team at the end of the meeting, all the key action items, who is responsible for each, and the due dates. It can sometimes be uncomfortable to reiterate and have to press certain people to confirm their dates. It may appear that you don't trust them, but if you don't confirm, you WILL get some unpleasant surprises. Confirming is no guarantee, but it does help, and it does send a message to everyone that you are expecting them to meet their commitments – and again, you are not demanding in a heavy-handed manner.

Summarizing the actions at the end of a meeting, or conference call with everyone present also adds some peer pressure because people are confirming and committing in front of the entire team, not only to you separately outside of the meeting.

Finally, send out the meeting minutes (create and use a template) with actions summary to the team via email so it is documented and you can reference it later if need be. And you will many times throughout the project.

After working together for a while, and you find that people are spot on with their tasks and areas of responsibility, you can lighten up, and this effort becomes less and less burdensome.

10. Daily project meetings.

Especially if you quickly need to get everyone in sync because there might be some confusion among members of the team, or mixed messages going to the customer, or maybe you are coming on to manage a project that is already underway, initiate daily morning meetings. I tended to start these meetings mid-morning like 9 am or 10 am to allow people time first thing in the morning to check on where things are, see if any issues came up since the day before, any notable progress, etc.

You may not win a lot of fans with initiating daily meetings, but I've found these to be absolutely critical in situations I just mentioned, and especially if the project is in trouble. Keep the meetings as short and as concise as possible, but make sure you get whatever information you need, like where people are, the major issues, etc., and get any of your directives or clarifying information out to make sure everyone has a common understanding on the key aspects of the project.

Very rarely, but a few times in critical situations, and for short periods of time, in addition to the morning meetings, I've had late afternoon update meetings, to assess progress, and if there were any glitches to resolve. Be on the look-out for people who may not feel comfortable bringing up issues in front of the entire team and have one-on-ones with them if necessary.

On the tracking of action items that I mentioned above in "Post-meeting actions summary," you'll need to be more selective in what you track because you'll likely not have time to track every item coming out of twice daily meetings, but you'll also be getting a daily view of project activities.

Cut your meetings back to twice a week or once per week, as soon as you feel comfortable that the team is moving in sync and making good progress.

11. Hold your customers accountable.

You need to be more diplomatic when dealing with your customer but whatever is agreed upon with them on the project up front is a commitment for both sides. If your customer had locked down and provided you with their requirements, and you've scoped, resourced, planned, scheduled, etc., and are well on your way on the project, you must hold firm on those requirements when requests for changes come, and it will not be easy to hold firm. It's a balancing act, but you will absolutely upset your customers sometimes by saying "no we can't add those new requirements, not without a corresponding resource and schedule adjustment."

If you instead choose not to upset your customer, because you simply can't say no, you will upset your people, and also lose revenue for your company. You, yes you, will be the reason your team will have to work harder and longer to get the project completed. Multiply that by how many times you knuckle under, and you'll have a serious morale problem and loss of your credibility.

It's a balancing act because you also don't want to lose the business. But what you'll also find is how often your customer responds to your "no we can't," in a surprising, reasonable way, because they are usually as reasonable as you are. If not, you stick to your position and let it get escalated up your management chain. They are in a better position to decide, or to review their portfolio of projects out there, to determine whether yours can have some flexibility.

What you've done though is to show your customer that at some point, you won't budge as the PM. Your customer may also not want the visibility of having to get their management pulled in again as well, so the next time they may come to you with changes and say, "OK, how much more time will you need to get these changes in?" That could be the start of a very good, mutually trusting, give and take, long-term working relationship.

If on the other hand, your customer is consistently unreasonable, then the relationship is probably a money-losing proposition because you won't only lose revenue, you'll lose some of your best people. But what also won't work is if you are always just a hard-ass, so again it's a balancing act, and there's give and take.

Just don't always give in, even if you have to say "no," then close your eyes and duck for cover. See what happens and work through it.

The more experience you have in these negotiations, the easier it gets.

CHAPTER 6:
WORST AND BEST

Among My Worst Experiences as a Manager

1. Satellite Center Closedown

In 2000 during another round of workforce reductions corporate-wide, I had to close-down our Satellite Center which was about 140 miles North of Los Angeles, and terminate the entire team of 20, including the Satellite Center Manager, who was a member of my management team. This was my worst experience as a manager, and by far the worst terminations I had to work through. It had a terrible impact on many people and their families, and I've never forgotten this.

To prepare for this closedown, the first thing I had to do, after struggling with what I was going to say and how I was going to say it, was to inform the Satellite Center Manager. I informed him that I needed to close the office, that I would have to separate his entire staff, and that I was going to have to terminate his employment as well. I then informed him of the date by which all of this needed to be completed. I also explained to him that I was hoping that he would stay and work with me during the entire process. I said that I would like his help with the turn-over of all their project work to the team at my home office, with the termination of each of his people, the closing down of the facility, terminating the lease, a number of other details, and then finally I would have to do his own separation from the company.

He was a trusted member of my management team, and a good friend, as all my managers were.

First thing in the morning of the closedown announcement to the team, I drove up, starting out at 5 am, and I met with the Center Manager off-site, to review our plan on what was about to take place. We then arrived at the office, and he called an all-hands meeting. Following the process and instructions that had been laid out, there was no heads-up to the team of the impending close-down, nor of my arriving there to make the announcement.

I had visited the Center on numerous occasions and had a very good relationship with the staff, having also joined them during recognition and happy hour events. As people started coming into the conference room, they sensed that something was ominous. I certainly couldn't greet them the same way as I normally did, knowing that in a few minutes, they would all learn that today was going to be their last day with the company. Waiting for everyone to arrive, people whom I knew and who were a part of my team, but in silence, felt like a lifetime.

After the hours spent preparing what I was going to say, which included things per guidance from corporate, I made the announcement to everyone. I also had to inform them that there was no option for a transfer to another location, even if there was a need. I had to keep it very short, taking minimal questions, then informing everyone that immediately, we will start calling each person for their formal separations, so to please return to their work areas and collect their personal items, then adjourned. We did not feel the need to have any security present, and it wasn't even a consideration.

After the announcement to the team, and although I was advised that it was not necessary and should probably not be involved, I sat through each termination. I was concerned that some people might be angry or maybe even furious, but not surprisingly everyone, except maybe one, was extremely professional, as they had always been. I felt that I needed to be there to show them respect and appreciation for their many years of dedication, hard work, and contributions to EDS.

It was the Satellite Center Manager who had to do the formal separations and the needed paperwork, but I wanted to be there to provide moral support because it was such a difficult thing to do with the impact on each person who he had worked with closely for many years. I did get to thank each one of them and wished them well.

I had also received corporate guidance that I should avoid saying "sorry" in the announcement to the team or in any of the individual separations because from a legal standpoint, it could have been interpreted by someone that we knew we were doing something wrong, particularly because it was in California.

The Satellite Center Manager was a good friend, and he could not have been more gracious and helpful, and dedicated to the well-being of his people during this awful time. He stayed through the entire ordeal, and we worked closely the entire time through the closing, and to his last day. He exemplified a management professional. I felt terrible how this all ended but was extremely fortunate to have him.

This was happening across the company, and I learned months later that a few managers who were let go in similar situations, like my Satellite Center Manager, found out that they themselves were being terminated only after they had completed the separation of all their people.

EDS corporate "layoffs", "down-sizing", "right-sizing", "realignments", "workforce reductions", "reduction in force (RIF)", started well before this Satellite Center close-down, it continued after the close down, and also after I had moved on from the SE Center where I no longer had any people responsibilities.

It was difficult to see and hear of really good people who were let go due to the realignments. I myself survived by somehow not being in the wrong place at the wrong time. But also when I was facing a layoff from the Sales group, having credibility with a friend and former center manager peer did, very fortunately, get me a transfer into the Government Services group. And even after that, it helped to not be on the bottom of team rankings, as layoffs continued, including in the Government Services group.

2. A Bad Joke

I was at the SE/Solution Center Managers' Division meeting at our Corporate Headquarters in Plano, Texas, one year. It happened to be about one month after I was promoted to the SoCal Account/Center manager position, so it was my first Division level meeting. At the adjournment of the last meeting of the day, and with the Center managers and our Division manager starting to get up, one of the older and more senior Center Managers throws out a joke to our Division manager but for all to hear, "hey, do you know why there will be a chill tomorrow? Because there will be a Nip in the air."

I had never heard that before but he was referencing the anniversary of the 1941 Japanese attack on Pearl Harbor which was a few weeks before. As a Japanese American, I was of course the only Asian in the room.

I remember giving a quarter laugh but catching myself. It was a reflex, I guess to not be rude when someone tries to crack a joke, but no one else uttered a sound. There was definite tension that filled the room, as everyone got up, gathered their things and silently walked out of the conference room. I know the others felt bad as the rest of us all got along really well, especially my former manager and mentor who was there, and our Division manager. I'm sure he didn't let that go, as he wasn't one to let anything slide, although he didn't say anything at the moment.

Growing up in Hawaii, I had a very sheltered life relative to things like this. I had been called a racial slur before, so knew how that felt, but this was very different, especially being in a professional setting and as the new guy among company colleagues.

Being generally good natured, and being in an unfamiliar situation, I didn't know how to react to that. I was pretty shell-shocked. So I can relate to people who, in very unusual or surprising situations, react in a way that on reflection, may have seemed very odd, or not fitting, and who wished they could have responded more appropriately at the time.

Later, of course, I thought of all the things I should have/could have said, but didn't, including offering to settle the matter outside, where he would have kicked my ass anyway, but at least it would have been up-and-up, face-to-face, but of course, suggesting that would have been just as unprofessional on my part.

But my biggest regret is that I didn't have the presence of mind to point out to him that I was a very proud son of a US Army veteran. My father was a proud American, which he instilled in me, and is laid to rest at the Veterans Cemetery in my hometown. As a side note, my father, who was a corporal, had missed the war but landed in Japan off a transport ship as part of the US Occupation Force. It was in 1947 that he was granted leave to travel from his base in Haneda to Naha, Okinawa to visit his sister, my aunt, and my cousins. He had taken up a collection from his unit and brought his sister a bag full of money to help them. They were still having a difficult time in the harsh post-war conditions.

This was the one and only time that I had ever experienced anything like this in my 32 plus years with the company. As a proud EDSer, I was actually embarrassed and ashamed that this could have happened in the company. I never mentioned or discussed this with anyone at work.

My Most Rewarding and Satisfying Aspects of Management

Being able to recognize people for their accomplishments and achievements, and getting to experience their reactions of pride and a sense of satisfaction for their hard work and contributions, were probably the most satisfying parts of my job as a manager. This includes one-on-one pats-on-the-back; recognizing people in team and account meetings; recognizing teams after a grueling project; awarding perks, bonuses, and salary increases; informing people of their promotions, announcing these in account meetings, etc.

It was also very rewarding to teach, train, and mentor up-and-coming leaders. Those who had that spark, who were eager to learn, and who really appreciated the advice and guidance. It was especially satisfying when some took the time to let me know that they appreciated that I was setting the example for people.

It also honestly felt very good to be looked up to and respected by people as the leader, or the person in charge. It started small as a team leader, then as a supervisor, then increasing as I moved up through several levels of management.

- Once when I was the account manager, I was on a conference call where the party on the other end, who was from another account, was being a little abrasive discussing a project issue until her coworker, who must have been sitting next to her, informed her in a hushed voice that she was talking to the account manager, where she quickly apologized and completely changed her tone.

- Another time when we received visitors from another account and the visiting manager walked right past, totally ignoring me to shake the hand of one of my managers who happened to be 6' tall, until he was told that I was "Norm" the account manager, then enthusiastically turned and shook my hand with a bright smile.

- Most importantly, however, is when you can see that you've earned some, and hopefully most, people's respect as a leader.

It's pretty big-headed of me to talk about having the corner office but here goes. As the account manager in the last office space that I occupied before transferring out of the SE Center, it was the one and only time that I had an office with windows looking outside of the building.

When we moved into this new office space, and while doing the buildout, I avoided taking this nice area in favor of making it a conference room, until one of my direct-report managers questioned why I wasn't taking this corner space as my office. She then got my other managers to insist that I take it. I did have the option to take this office space, but I didn't want the appearance that I was grabbing a plum spot for myself simply because I was the center manager. I did eventually take this corner office, but felt extremely touched and honored that those who were my right-hand people, and whom I so depended upon every day, pushed for this.

As the person in charge, it also felt good to sit at the head of the conference room table in our leadership meetings with about ten managers at its peak. Then to be the one to make the final decisions if necessary (most were by consensus), that impacted so many people, and to make a positive impact more often than not. If it were the other way around, I would not have been in that management position for very long. Of course, you always have the pressure of the job, and your reputation is on the line with every decision. But it was the absolute highest point in my career, having the management and administrative team that I had, in the final few years before transferring out.

Each one of them was caring, professional, 100% reliable, we had been through many extreme highs and deep lows together, and we considered each other good friends. I'm glad that I told most of them at that time, hopefully all, that because of them, this was the pinnacle of my career with EDS.

There were many other rewarding aspects of the job including improving overall productivity and getting the entire SE Center to SEI CMM Level 2, and close to Level 3, which was a huge deal back in the 1990's. It was also satisfying to consistently meet our financial targets, and with "stretch" goals, but that was a double-edged sword because as an SE Center, we were an expense as opposed to a profit center. And having many SE Centers across the country, being in Los Angeles, we had the highest expenses due to California's higher salary ranges, lease rates for office space, utility costs, etc., so we stood out like a sore thumb.

We were the "ugly duckling" among the SE centers from a financial standpoint. On top of that was the fact that we were "Southern California," home of the glitz and glamor of Hollywood, where some thought our SEs were a bunch of prima donnas, and yup, I heard it myself. Furthermore, through California's law, we lit the fuse for all of EDS in the US to have to change its strict professional dress code to allow women to wear the pantsuit, but that's a whole different story.

Here are some added details on the financials if you're interested.

In the mid-1990s, EDS Corporate went to a standard rate for SE Centers, meaning one billing rate per hour per resource level (for SE, Senior SE, etc.) to represent every Center. So regardless as to each Centers' operational expenses, which varied widely across the country, this meant that for the SE Centers in the low expense areas of the country, the billing rate would allow them to recover significantly more than their total expenses, or "over-recover," where they appeared highly profitable.

In Southern California, in contrast, because our SE Center had among, if not the highest expenses in the nation, we always "under-recovered," or showed that we were operating at a loss. It didn't matter to some that it was in the math and evened out in the roll-up. We were still the expensive Center that drove up the rates for everyone.

But far and away, being able to acknowledge, recognize, and reward people for their teamwork, for helping and supporting their customers, and for their good as well as exceptional work were the most rewarding, and something I could do most frequently. This was done face-to-face, with thank you notes, cards, emails (there was no texting back then), phone calls, in team meetings, large gatherings, etc.

Below is an example of a letter I sent to the parents of one of my top performers. I was still a relatively new SE Manager at the time with several SE Supervisors reporting to me. I had sent letters like this to parents of employees several times. I had not considered at the time, what an indelible impact this could have. Although this individual moved on to new and greater things with EDS, we crossed paths a number of times, and he reminded me a few times how much he and his parents still appreciated this letter, even twenty years later.

Part of the reason that I wrote this letter to his parents was that I had lost my parents when I was only in my early twenties, and I was touched that they had a very close relationship.

December 16, 1991

B███ and P███████
██████████ Drive
██████, CA ████

Dear Mr. and Mrs. ████████,

There have been very few occasions where I have been inspired to write the parents of someone who works for me. This happens to be such an occasion. I wanted you to know that your son, ████, is a top performer at our EDS Systems Engineering Center and that you have every reason to be proud of him. I'm his manager, and I've seen him, first-hand, excel to become one of our top Systems Engineers, and now, one of our organization's key leaders.

I'm sure you know by now that ████ has recently been promoted to Systems Engineering Supervisor, a position for which he has earned with distinction. It is evident to me and to the other managers here, that ████ stands out as a leader. He is also a role model with his demonstrated commitment and dedication to his projects, his team-members, and this organization. ████ continues to eagerly accept increasingly greater responsibilities. He also demonstrates strength of character in dealing with very difficult situations, all the while maintaining his great can-do attitude. ████ has become a very strong and polished leader. Much of my accomplishments can be attributed to the efforts of ████ who has become one of my trusted "right-hand" people.

In addition to these strengths and achievements, I've recognized that ████ has the warmth of a person with a good heart. I can see this in the way that he takes care of his people, and in the way he shows his care of his family, ████ and the kids, and you, his parents. I admire these values, I simply like and respect ████ as a person because of them, and I'm certain it reflects on the way he was raised and on the support that he gets from ████.

I feel extremely fortunate to have ████ working with me. He is going to have a great future with the company and I'd choose to be on his team in a second. It is because he often speaks of you, that I wanted to share this.

I wish you a Merry Christmas and a Happy New Year!

With warm regards,

Norm Oshiro

Anaheim SE Center
Suite ████
████ North State College Boulevard
Orange, California 92668
(714) ████████

CHAPTER 7: CLOSING

My First Big Break

In 1971, soon after I switched majors from Engineering to Sociology due to poor grades, I got a huge break. One of my best high school and surfing friends who was a Biology major, and who was working as a Teaching Assistant in that department – who today has a very successful Veterinary Hospital in Honolulu – gave me the heads-up that the UH Meteorology Department was looking for a part-time student research assistant at their Cloud Physics Observatory there on the Hilo campus. His tip ultimately changed the course of my life. This job sounded so different and so interesting that I latched on to it.

Up to that point, I had been working at my relative's Service Station, where I had started years before I could even legally drive. I don't know what got into me, but I took a shot and applied even though I was totally unqualified. I had long hair that was bleached orange from all the sun and surfing, I wore a headband at times, was a grubby dresser like a typical surfer in the '70s, and I had a poor academic record both from High School and currently at the University.

Although my grades were on a recent upswing, my only work experience was working at the service station where I was still employed. I was interested in science but certainly wasn't any good in math or physics. But, I was really interested in the job, really wanted to do what seemed like different and fascinating work, and I demonstrated my desire through persistence. Instead of mailing in the application, I hand-delivered it to the Observatory office which was on the upper part of the University campus. At the in-person interview, I showed up early and waited for my turn. Then to follow up, instead of calling, I visited the office in person, surfboard strapped to my racks atop my car, to ask how things were going and if I needed to provide any additional information.

When asked to call in for an update or decision on a certain date, rather than call, I showed up in person to inquire. I did this at least twice after the initial interview. I eventually and excitedly found that I actually got the job, beating out many much more qualified students. I found out later that I even bettered someone who was later nominated and went to West Point. The Observatory Director told me that it was my personal interest, desire, friendly attitude, and persistence that motivated him to select me.

Dr. Charles M. Fullerton, who was the director of the observatory, through the next three years, and through his unselfish and frequent pats-on-the-back, encouragement and support, and even enthusiastic praise of my work products, made a significant impact on me.

Every workday, I couldn't wait to get to work because of all the new things I was learning and doing, and because of the camaraderie and friendships that I developed there. Dr. Fullerton eventually encouraged me to apply to Graduate School in Meteorology, even though I had dropped out from an Engineering major and was getting a BA in Sociology, a discipline that I turned out to love, but which did not require any of the advanced hard sciences in Math and Physics. He recommended me to his boss, the Meteorology Department Chairman, Dr. Colin Ramage, at the time, at UH Manoa on Oahu. It was only through Dr. Fullerton's recommendation that I was accepted into Graduate School. He was one of the people who significantly changed the course of my life. I was extremely fortunate to have such a role model and mentor.

I learned from example after example that supporting and encouraging people helps to give them the drive to excel. His leadership and guidance motivated and inspired me to achieve things far beyond what I ever thought was possible for myself.

So with grad school on the horizon, I signed up for classes in Calculus and Physics, including summer classes to catch up, and to my surprise I did OK. An important point here is that although I once thought that maybe I did not have the intellect to do math and physics, I found that I was indeed able to. It was just timing, interest, and having a different mental attitude that was different. Oh, and by spending much more time working for it by actually studying hard!

Then there was the move to Oahu in 1973, moving into the dorm at UH Manoa, and that first semester in Meteorology Grad School. I can still remember my first day sitting in Theoretical Meteorology with my BA in Sociology, never having taken a class in Meteorology, and with everyone else in the class having a BS in Meteorology. It was a shocker – like a 2x4 across the head. But that's another story.

At least I was now on a path that was preparing me for the career that I would eventually have.

Major Influencers

1. Dr. Charles M. Fullerton, Director, Cloud Physics Observatory, the University of Hawaii at Hilo.

Dr. Fullerton's hiring of me in 1971 as a student research assistant for the Cloud Physics Observatory, ultimately led to a new outlook and direction for the future and put me onto an actual career path. I was pretty much a surf bum at the time, but his endless support, pats-on-the-back, and encouragement inspired me; and his recommendation which led to my acceptance into the Department of Meteorology's graduate program changed my life.

2. Yoshio Obasa

In 1972 I was still a long-haired, sloppy dressing surfer going to college. All of my friends and fellow surfers also had long hair. I always wanted to learn the Okinawan martial art, since that was my heritage but was too carefree and lazy to get started. I was told that my grandfather on my father's side was quite proficient at this but had passed away before I was born. I found a school that taught this Okinawan art but the instructor was known to be extremely hard and strict. He was Obasa Sensei with the Shorinji Kempo Ryu Son Ryu. But even worse, I would have to cut my hair very short – I mean, I would have to become a "square." After many months of soul searching, I finally decided to take the plunge. It was a huge sacrifice for me, and it caused terrible embarrassment for me to have short hair among my peers and surfing friends for a couple of years until I got over it. But it turned out to be one of the best decisions of my life. I never got to a high level, but I was there long enough to learn about respect, discipline, coordination and balance, centering and breathing, and meditation. I found it amazing to learn that being calm made you more alert, and being relaxed allowed you to move faster. The breadth of his teachings made a huge impact on better preparing me for many aspects of my life.

> *One day at practice, an extremely drunk man came in and with slurred speech, was acting up and kept yelling that he wanted to fight. Obasa sensei, first took off his worn and*

tattered belt, then walked over to the man to talk to him in a very calm and polite manner. He was there for several minutes, in no hurry, calmed the man down, and eventually helped him outside. We then continued with our practice as though nothing had happened. He showed humility, understanding, and compassion towards this troubled person.

3. **EDS**

   - Egon Petersen
     - The EDS manager who first hired me into the company in Honolulu in 1983, and who was the first example of the type of encouraging, caring, professional, and ethical leader I was to find throughout my career with EDS.

   - Mary Buretta – see Book Dedication

   - Nancy Boyer-Castro
     - She was the account manager for the Anaheim SE Center in Southern California, who transferred me in from Seattle. She was a mentor who stretched me to achieve ever-increasing levels of responsibility, influence, and leadership in my career. She was focused, detailed, disciplined, and also very caring and compassionate.

   - Chuck Walton
     - Took over for Nancy as the account manager. A warm and caring leader, a teacher and mentor, and whose encouragement and persistence allowed me to attain my highest management level in EDS, which was managing the Southern California SE/Solution Center.

   - Mia Morris
     - Dedicated, hardworking, efficient, accurate, professional, courteous and considerate to everyone, and my trusted Administrative and Financials Assistant at the SE Center.

4. Cousin Byron – see Book Dedication.

Byron and my son back in Hawaii.

Career Chronology

Year	Age	Description
1969	17	Graduated from Hilo High School & started college.
1971	19	Hired as a student research assistant by the University of Hawaii, Meteorology Department's Cloud Physics Observatory, UH Hilo.
1973	21	BA in Sociology (Inter-Ethnic Relations) from UH Hilo, and started Graduate School in Meteorology at UH Manoa (Honolulu).
1973	22	Winter, dropped out of Grad School and returned to Hilo due to my mother's death. My father had passed away seven months earlier. Reemployed by the Cloud Physics Observatory at UH Hilo.
1974	22	Returned to Grad School at Manoa and worked as a research assistant for the Meteorology Department in wind energy until I graduated.
1977	25	Graduated MS Meteorology, and was hired as the Meteorology Field Manager for Hawaii's statewide wind energy potential research until 1982.
1983	31	Hired by Electronic Data Systems (EDS) as a computer programmer. (At that time, EDS had about 12,000 employees. It was 8,000 in 1979.)
1985	34	EDS lost the Region's government contract, so we were presented with a choice to hire on with the new contractor and continue work, or try to find another position with EDS which meant moving somewhere on the mainland. I was offered and accepted a transfer to the Seattle SE Center in WA. While there I was promoted from Systems Engineer (SE) to SE Supervisor. • SE Centers, in a nutshell, provided IT resources anytime, anywhere, and for any duration.
1986	35	Transferred to the Anaheim SE Center (ASEC) in Southern California. (GM buys out Ross

		Perot. At that time, EDS had about 44,000 employees with the ramp up to support GM, who became our new owner as of 1984.)
		Following are SE Center name changes that were corporate driven. I use mostly "SE Center" in the book to avoid confusion. • 1986 – When I arrived was the Anaheim SE Center (ASEC). • 1991 – Anaheim Development Center (ADC). • 1992 – Anaheim Technical Delivery Solution Center (ATDSC). • 1993 – Southern California Development Center (SCDC). • 1995 – Southern California Resource Center (SCRC). • 1998 – Southern California Solution Centre (SCSC).
1990	38	Promoted to SE Manager.
1992	40	Manager for a commercial IT business EDS acquired from McDonnell Douglas Systems Integration (MDSI) for one year.
1993	41	Acting Account Manager for the Southern California SE Center.
1994	42	Promoted to Account Manager (approximately 75 total staff and $7M annual budget).
1997	46	The SE Center was assessed/certified as an SEI CMM Level 2 maturity IT organization. (EDS had approximately 110,000 employees. GM had spun off EDS in 1996.)
1998	46	Promoted to Technical Delivery Organization Manager.
1999	47	Completed 22-month Executive MBA program (Class XIII) at the University of Southern California (USC), Marshall School of Business, while working full time.
2000	48	Following EDS consolidations, total SE Center staff grew to 192.

2000	49	Joined EDS Sales, in Sales Support. (EDS had approximately 130,000 employees in about 50 countries.)
2002	51	Due to layoffs in Sales, joined EDS Government Services Group to support the US Navy as a Project Manager in San Diego, CA.
2005	54	Promoted to Project Manager – Advanced.
2008	57	EDS purchased by HP. (At the time EDS had approximately 139,000 employees in 64 countries.)
2009	58	Promoted to Customer Project/Program Manager – Expert.
2011	60	ITIL V3 Foundation Certification, (ITIL: Information Technology Infrastructure Library).
2013	61	PMI PMP credentialed (PMI: Project Management Institute, PMP: Project Management Professional).
2015	63	Accepted early retirement offer and retired after 32 plus years with EDS/HP.

EDS Leadership Training classes attended (partial list)

- Introduction to Leadership, 1985
- Basic Leadership, 1985
- Leadership Application Workshop, 1988
- Financial Controls Course, 1988
- Performance Appraisal Workshop, 1988
- Compensation Workshop, 1988
- Account Leaders Course, 1989
- Accounting And Finance For Non-Financial Leaders, 1989
- Values In Action, 1992
- Diversity - Valuing & Managing, 1992
- Conflict Management, 1995
- Behavioral Interviewing, 1995
- Executive Relationship Building, 2000
- Leading People Through Performance Management, 2000
- Workplace Harassment For Individual Performers, 2002
- Selling Essentials, 2002
  - Strategic Value Selling
  - Executive Relationship Building
  - Helping Clients Succeed

EDS Open Door Policy

"Open Door Policy Concept: The Open Door Policy Is Critically Important In Companies Who Have Large Degrees Of Management Discretion."

1. It is the employee's decision to utilize the open door policy.
2. The employee is entitled to utilize the open door policy.
3. There should be no retribution for executing the open door policy.
4. It is a management obligation to support the open door policy.
5. It provides an opportunity for the manager to review objectively, and understand the employee's concerns.
6. It does not guarantee that the answer will be the one that satisfies everyone.
7. The employee has the option to go up the chain of command using the open door policy.
8. The manager should assist the employee with the next level of the chain.

Note, as I wrote earlier in the book about EDS' Open Door Policy: It was always impressed upon us to make employees aware of this policy, to encourage its use, and that the consequence would be severe if any leader impeded its use. To be clear, we understood that if a manager prevented an employee from using the Open Door Policy in any way, or inflicted retribution on anyone using the Open Door Policy, they would be fired on the spot.

EDS' Grass Roots Wisdoms

(From EDS' 3-Day Leadership Application Workshop (LAW), January 1988.)

Grass Roots Wisdoms:

- Be upfront, blunt, and candid.
- Managers are not obligated to perpetuate foolishness.
- Managers are in charge, not the employees.
- Managers must choose which problem to live with.
- People need to see the scoreboard.
- Run the company so the best people love it.
- If people don't do what I want, it's my fault (you get what you tolerate).
- Get all the liars in the same room.
- Get out your own checkbook.
- Sit in the grandstands.
- Bad news doesn't improve with age.
- No second chance for a first impression.

Suggested Reading: **Old School Leadership Wisdoms**, 2016, by my friend and colleague Gary R. Hassenstab, for a detailed discussion on EDS' Grass Roots Wisdoms. Earlier in this book, under "Uncomfortable," where I had expressed my reluctance to accept the Account Manager position, Gary was the manager that I referenced who I thought was better qualified for the job. He was always a valued colleague and supporter and later joined EDS' Leadership Development Program at corporate headquarters in Plano, TX to train new leaders, and then became a coach for EDS' Executive Development Program.

Additional EDS Words of Wisdom:

- Always operate within the ethical bull's-eye.
- Never operate on the fringes of ethical behavior.
- Don't do things that would even appear to be unethical.

- Always look at what you are doing, or planning to do, and consider how it would look if it were reported on the evening news.
- No alcohol consumption on the job, even if the customer does.
- Select the person who has earned the opportunity and who is the best person for the job.
- Never transfer a problem.
- When facing a problem or a crisis, be able to 'huddle' with frank and open discussions, then embrace and carry out as one team and one voice, the final play that's called.
  - The train is headed North – are you getting on it?
- See snake, kill snake.
  - Sometimes you simply won't have time to pull a committee together, brainstorm alternatives, prioritize, and then finalize a solution.
- There are rules and guidelines but as an EDS leader, always be willing to exercise management discretion.
- Sometimes it's better to beg for forgiveness rather than ask for permission.
- Demonstrate healthy discontent.
- Choose your battles – best not to argue on everything.

Some Words of Wisdom while Growing up in Hawaii

The following are just a few words of wisdom that come to mind from my growing up in Hawaii, and which helped to shape my life-long outlook and behavior. These words come out naturally for me in pidgin, like: "ehh, no ack bossee!" or "no sho off!" But in regular English, here are some of these wisdoms:

- Don't act bossy – don't talk down to people and order them around.
- Don't show off.
- Don't get cocky.
- Don't make fun of people.
- Don't talk back.
- Follow the rules.
- When people are trying their best, cut them some slack.
- Be fair.
- Be a good sport.
- Show some Aloha:
  - Be friendly.
  - Be respectful.
  - Be helpful.
  - Show that you care.
- Don't let people push you around or treat you badly.
- If somebody gives you the stink eye: "eh, waht you looking at?!"

Criticisms of EDS

I wanted to make a few comments about how EDS was viewed in the press by industry analysts for many years before, and even after HP acquired us in 2008. I didn't want to ignore the elephant in the room relative to the criticisms of EDS at that time where simultaneously, continuous rounds of layoffs were occurring.

It's been years ago now, but as a significant example, a former HP CEO's purchase of EDS in 2008 was viewed by many analysts as being one of the worst and most disastrous acquisitions in the technology industry, if not the worst. EDS had been severely criticized in the press for underperforming for years, well before that acquisition, and the criticisms continued until what remained of EDS, HP Enterprise Services, was spun off and merged with Computer Sciences Corporation to form DXC Technology in 2017. This was almost two years after I had already retired as a proud former EDS employee, and also, as a proud HP employee (still treasure my working RPN HP-35 from 1973 and still refuse to own any other brand).

I can't speak to the analysts' criticisms from an EDS corporate financials and performance viewpoint, but I do have a perspective as one of many thousands who worked in the EDS and HPES trenches.

> *Humor me here, but I think that a scene from one of my favorite movies "The Secret Life of Walter Mitty" captures my sense of those years quite well. The scene is at the end of the movie after Walter had been laid off along with many of his friends and co-workers. Following all the layoffs, he walks in on a meeting being held by the manager from corporate who had executed the down-sizing, and who had been extremely arrogant and disrespectful to people even as he fired many of them.*
>
> *Walter (Ben Stiller) points out to him that yes, I understand that you have your marching orders, and you have to do what you have to do, but, when you come in and push people out, you should also know that these people worked **really hard** to build this company (the movie was about Life magazine).*

I recognize the importance of increasing shareholder value. So maybe our corporate executives, including the board, didn't do a good enough job, and EDS probably deserved the criticism – the numbers seemed to justify it. But in the trenches, I saw with my own eyes, over my entire three decades with the company, dedicated people working hard every day, often working really really hard, doing quality work, and doing their level best to support their customers and teammates to meet their deadlines. Hard work and commitment like this helped to build this 4-person company in 1962 to almost 140,000 employees in 2008.

Like thousands of fellow-EDSers, I was a survivor of some very harsh times in my stretch with the company, and I'll always remember that there were thousands more who were just as dedicated and who worked just as hard, and even harder, but who did not survive the cutbacks.

Bibliography

- EDS Corporate Ethics: A Code of Conduct, Your Responsibility, 1983
- EDS 21 Steps Leadership Development, 1986.
- EDS Leading People, Fifth Edition, Revised February 1992, Copyright 1988, Electronic Data Systems, EDS Private.
- A Guide to the Project Management Body of Knowledge (PMBOK Guide), Fourth Edition, Copyright 2008, by Project Management Institute (PMI) – note that if you are planning to be PMP credentialed, exam preparation will require the latest edition.
- Rita Mulcahy's PMP Exam Prep, by Rita Mulcahy, Seventh Edition, Copyright 2011, RMC Publications, Inc. – note that if you are planning to be PMP credentialed, exam preparation will require the latest edition.
- Old School Leadership Wisdoms (EDS Grass Roots Wisdoms of Leadership), Gary Hassenstab, 2016. (Gary is an EDS colleague and friend of mine. See my Grass Roots Wisdoms Section.)

Closing

About the Author

Norm Oshiro has a BA in Sociology (inter-ethnic relations specialty) and an MS in Meteorology, both from the University of Hawaii (UH). He has an MBA from the University of Southern California (USC), Marshall School of Business, and is also credentialed as a Project Management Professional (PMP) through the Project Management Institute (PMI). He spent 11 years in meteorology field research and co-authored four UH research papers on Hawaii wind energy assessments, then spent 32 years advancing through the ranks with Electronic Data Systems (EDS) and Hewlett Packard (HP), which acquired EDS in 2008, both large multinational information technology (IT) corporations.

Norm started with EDS in 1983 as a computer programmer/systems engineer (SE), then was moved into the role as a team leader, then promoted to SE supervisor, SE manager, then moved up to manage an organization and team of SE managers as the account manager for EDS' Southern California Solution Center. After seven years in the center manager role, to broaden his corporate skill-set, he transferred into the Sales organization providing sales support for two years until there was a large corporate sales force reduction, where he then transferred into the Government Services group and progressively advanced as a Project Manager until his retirement in 2015.

He was born and raised in Hilo, on the Big Island of Hawaii, where he grew up in a multi-cultural neighborhood and community. His next-door neighbors were Hawaiian, Portuguese, Filipino, and Japanese, and also had Caucasian, Korean, and Chinese friends through school and sports. Starting with T-ball and Pop Warner, he played team sports to his teen years, then became pretty much of a surf bum from high school into college.

His grandparents on both sides, emigrated from Okinawa, Japan to work in the sugar plantations. He's considered Sansei, or third generation in the US. His mother was an office worker at a collection agency for many years, and his father worked for Aloha Airlines for 25 years. In their younger days, his mother and two of her sisters were traditional Okinawan dancers who performed at celebrations and community events, and his father was a boxer. Norm learned cool-headed calmness from his father, and not to take sh*t from anyone from his mother. She never told him to do any such thing, but he learned from observation. She was tiny but not afraid to confront and argue with anyone if they were rude or did something she didn't think was right.

Norm never did that well in the classroom from elementary through high school, including his first two years in college, until a mentor finally got him inspired to reach for a better future.

Thank you! I sincerely hope this book helps you to achieve greater success in your career – whichever path you choose.

– Norm

CPSIA information can be obtained
at www.ICGtesting.com
Printed in the USA
LVHW101950250320
651176LV00006B/349